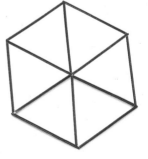

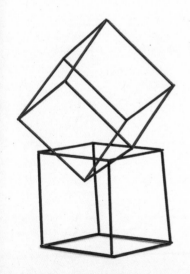

BRIT
INSURANCE
DESIGNS OF
THE YEAR

DESIGN
MUSEUM

Curator
ALEX NEWSON

Project management
MELANIE SPENCER

Exhibition design
DAVID KOHN ARCHITECTS

Graphic design
MULTISTOREY // ROBERT GREEN

Editor
ANNA FAHERTY

Additional photography and digital manipulation
PEER LINDGREEN

The Design Museum would like to thank all the nominators and nominees
who have helped deliver Brit Insurance Designs of the Year 2011.

Published by
DESIGN MUSEUM
Shad Thames
London
SE1 2YD
United Kingdom
designmuseum.org

ISBN-10: 1 87200 530 0
ISBN-13: 978 1 87200 530 0

Now in their fourth year, the Brit Insurance Design Awards have become a hugely anticipated feature of the international design calendar. The diversity of winners in the first three years – Yves Béhar and fuseproject's One Laptop per Child, Shepard Fairey's Barack Obama poster and Min-Kyu Choi's folding three-pin plug – demonstrate both the scope of the awards and design's potential to transform for the better the way we live and interact with others. In the case of the folding plug, the concept has progressed from prototype in 2010 to the reality of mass manufacture in 2011.

Among this year's nominations the ripple effects of the global downturn remain very much in evidence. Sustainability and efficiency continue as themes running through many of the projects, while the interactive category suggests that 2010 belonged to the app. The Awards jury, headed by Stephen Bayley, will be asked to judge the best of each of seven design categories and declare an overall winner from what is again a strong, diverse and thought-provoking shortlist.

DANE DOUETIL CBE
Chief Executive, Brit Insurance

CONTENTS

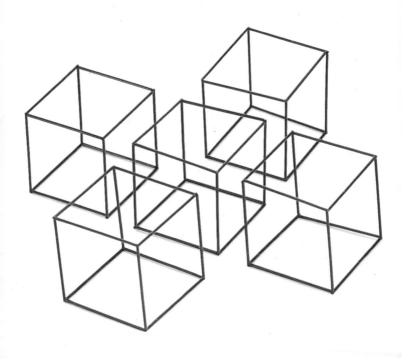

With the help of a dedicated group of internationally renowned design experts the Design Museum has compiled a shortlist of almost 100 projects reflecting the finest design from the past year. Split across seven design disciplines – architecture, fashion, furniture, graphics, interactive, product and transport – these ground-breaking projects aptly illustrate the widening scope of design and its increasingly influential role in shaping society.

By offering support to entire communities or providing life-saving solutions for developing countries, many of these designs fulfil this role literally. Others are less conspicuous in their impact but offer equally important solutions to aspects of daily life, such as seating, transport and general comfort. In addition to the many commendable social projects, innovations and grand gestures, the importance of beauty should not be forgotten, as it too can have a transformative effect. A select jury of experts have the difficult task of choosing winners from each of these seven design disciplines, along with an award for the overall best design.

It is fascinating to see how the character and feel of the shortlist changes from year to year, highlighting current trends in both design and a wider visual culture. Reflecting this, the 2011 physical exhibition is orientated around five main themes: city, play, learn, home and share. These themes are reflective of this year's designs, as championed by our group of nominators. However, this is just one approach to grouping the projects, and in this publication the nominations are presented within the established award categories.

One noticeable trend is the emergence of the iPad and other tablet devices. Advances in portable touch screen technology have produced an accessible new archetype which is leading innovation in content, design and the human interface for applications. The continued presence of sustainable and environmental design is also apparent. However, rather than being treated as an exclusive factor, sustainable elements are now frequently embedded within the design process – an indicator that sustainability is becoming the rule rather than the exception. As you browse the nominated works you will no doubt find alternative themes and patterns emerging.

ALEX NEWSON
Curator, Design Museum

ARCHITECTURE

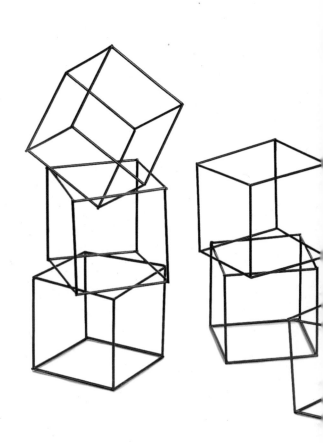

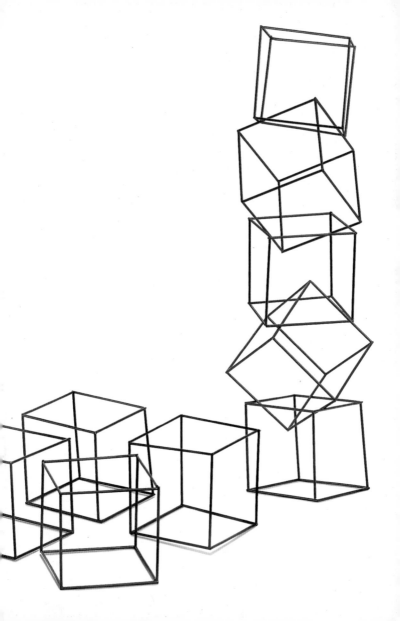

1111 LINCOLN ROAD
MIAMI BEACH

Envisioned by ROBERT WENNETT
Designed by HERZOG & DE MEURON

☆ Nominated by RAYMUND RYAN: "1111 Lincoln Road is a radical rethinking of that most conventional of typologies, the stacked parking garage. An open arrangement is achieved by elevating the permissible number of parking trays to occupy the full volume of the site and by propping these slabs on skinny piers. The slab perimeter and cable balustrades are also kept to an absolute minimum. With the street level allocated to retail, the topmost floor hosts an extraordinary penthouse apartment and a dramatic sloping garden. Boutiques and other leisure facilities can be accommodated in simple glass enclosures throughout the structure, while the decks are used for temporary musical, cultural and social events, as well as parking. Engineering, urban massing, careful detailing, and a playful dispersal of programme make for a unique and active urban element." — RR

1111lincolnroad.com

IMAGE © IWAN BAAN AND MBEACH1, LLLP

This mixed-use development is a fully open concrete structure combining retail and residential space with a car park. A public facility where people change from one mode of transportation to another, the building is particularly important in the Lincoln Road area, one of few locations in Miami where pedestrians take precedence over vehicles. With a retail unit and private residence located on the upper levels, the structure can also be used for parties, photo or film shoots, fashion shows, concerts and other social or commercial activities, all offering amazing views as a backdrop. Ceiling heights vary between standard parking height and double, or even triple, height in order to accommodate different programmes. An unenclosed, sculptural staircase in the centre provides pedestrians walking through the garage with a panoramic, ceremonial experience.

A FOREST FOR A MOON DAZZLER

GUANACASTE

BENJAMIN GARCIA SAXE

☆ Nominated by LUCY BULLIVANT: "Personal narrative and dreams of a better life drove Benjamin's design for a dwelling for his mother in the rainforest. This bamboo sanctuary is open plan, secure and intimately connected with its lush environment. When Helen first left the city for a more peaceful life she built a living space out of tree trunks, mosquito nets, tin and plastic bags, positioning her bed where she could watch the moon and recall memories of her sons. Benjamin reinterpreted her self-made dwelling, providing a view of the moon at a build cost of £24,000. An affordable space for an idyll many would envy — and more of us will need to find ways to create in the future — A Forest For a Moon Dazzler is their own sustainable home, a beautiful 'forest' of bamboo in a rainforest location." — LB

benjamingarciasaxe.com

IMAGE © ANDRES GARCIA LACHNER

Designed as a self-build house for the architect's mother, Benjamin Garcia Saxe's A Forest For a Moon Dazzler offers sanctuary away from the city. Under an umbrella tin roof, the bamboo cone ceiling opens up to the sky, providing constant links to the building's environment. The design addresses the client's practical and safety requirements, while the beautiful home — including a bedroom with a view of the moon — satisfies her emotional needs. Created from two identical living modules, the building is inexpensive and easy to construct. These modules are able to grow and multiply, creating an array of adaptable configurations which has sparked interest from government agencies considering low-cost housing options in developing countries. The construction might also be used for public schools in deprived areas of Latin America and other tropical locations.

BALANCING BARN
SUFFOLK

MVRDV
Co-architect: MOLE ARCHITECTS
Client: LIVING ARCHITECTURE

☆ Nominated by SAM HECHT: "Radical architecture built for anyone to experience in the form of a holiday let. What a wonderful idea. And in England! This can't be true… but it is. As part of the Living Architecture programme, anyone can experience this progressive home for a few days, and get inside the minds of MVRDV. It's not an image or a rendering – it's a real building in the landscape and you don't have to get on a plane to see it." — SH

mvrdv.nl

IMAGE © EDMUND SUMNER

Balancing Barn is the first completed building for Living Architecture, a not-for-profit initiative that offers the public the chance to rent houses designed by leading architects, with the purpose of promoting world-class modern architecture. Situated on a beautiful site by a small lake in the English countryside, the traditional shape and reflective metal sheeting take their references from the local building vernacular. In this sense the construction supports Living Architecture's aims of re-evaluating the countryside and making modern architecture accessible. On approach, the barn looks like a small, two-person house. At the end of the track, visitors suddenly experience the full 30m length and the spectacular cantilever. Extending 15m over a slope, the house plunges headlong into nature, where the surrounding landscape accentuates the sensation of the building's weightlessness.

BURJ KHALIFA
DUBAI

SKIDMORE, OWINGS & MERRILL LLP (SOM)
Client: EMAAR PROPERTIES PJSC

☆ Nominated by GUY NORDENSON: "The Burj Khalifa tower is over 60 per cent taller than the next highest building in the world. This is a measure not only of the aspirations of Dubai but, more importantly, of the accomplishment of the engineers and architects. SOM engineer William Baker designs to 'confuse the wind', using an engineering approach previously pioneered on projects such as the Jin Mao tower in Shanghai and the unbuilt 7 South Dearborn tower in Chicago. With the buttressed-core Y-shaped plan and the spiralling arrangement of setbacks, the structure robustly resists and deftly dodges the winds. Rumour has it that the tower was initially designed to be about 20 per cent shorter but well after construction began the client asked if Baker could add 100m, then another 60. Incredibly, with the help of wind engineer Peter Irwin, Baker managed to do so. Perhaps even now it is still growing." — GN

som.com

IMAGE © SOM // NICK MERRICK // HEDRICH BLESSING

With Burj Khalifa, the architects and engineers from the Chicago office of Skidmore, Owings & Merrill LLP (SOM) redefined what's possible with super-tall buildings. At the centre of a new city neighbourhood, Burj Khalifa incorporates references to Islamic architecture while reflecting the modern global community it will serve. The building's Y-shaped plan provides the maximum perimeter for windows in living spaces without developing unusable internal areas. As the tapering tower rises, setbacks occur at the ends of each wing, and the upward spiralling pattern decreases in mass as the height increases — a design which was modelled in a wind tunnel to minimise wind forces. Standing tall at 828m, Burj Khalifa holds the three building records of highest architectural top, highest occupied floor and highest tip, as recognised by the Council on Tall Buildings and Urban Habitat.

CONCRETE CANVAS SHELTERS

CONCRETE CANVAS (PETER BREWIN // WILLIAM CRAWFORD // PHILLIP GREER)

☆ Nominated by HUIB VAN DER WERF: "In our present global situation, architecture and design can actively contribute to tackling the effects of famine, disease, natural disasters and violent conflicts. Concrete Canvas Shelters provide a durable yet flexible temporary solution to a variety of international emergencies. The project is a fine example of architects and designers implementing innovation in order to actually make a difference." — HVDW

concretecanvas.co.uk

IMAGE © CONCRETE CANVAS

Peter Brewin and William Crawford conceived a new approach to cheap and rapid building construction while they were still at university. Using raw materials extremely efficiently, their design combines an inflatable inner liner and a unique outer fabric impregnated with dry concrete powder. Once inflated, the curved surface is optimised for compressive loading and the outside layer simply needs water to cause it to harden. The concept developed into Concrete Canvas Shelters, a range of structures requiring only water and air for construction. Deployed by two untrained people in under an hour and ready for use in 24 hours, the finished buildings are sterile, durable, fire-proof, thermally insulated and secure. The rapid construction time makes them ideal for humanitarian emergencies as well as a range of military and commercial operations.

LADAKH COMMONWEALTH PEACE PAVILION AND CLASSROOM INITIATIVE

SERGIO PALLERONI // BASIC INITIATIVE

☆ Nominated by CYNTHIA SMITH: "War wages all around this small Tibetan village nestled in the Himalayas. Afghanistan and Pakistan are both less than 150km away, and material from parachutes used in local conflicts makes its way onto the black market to be repurposed into peace tents and outdoor classrooms for local children. Built in the award-winning Druk White Lotus School grounds, these outdoor tensile structures are based on traditional Ladakhi yak hair tents, which resist wind and the extreme climate and incorporate local weaving and dyeing. These humble temporary classrooms reflect local nomadic herding culture, capturing the imagination and aspirations of the children. For the engineers and architects who designed and built the tents, they offer hope for a conflict-free world." — CS

ladakh.basicinitiative.com

IMAGE © BASIC INITIATIVE

The Commonwealth Peace Pavilion is an outdoor classroom space used by the Druk White Lotus School in Ladakh and its surrounding community. Located 4000m above sea level, the structure provides sanctuary from the intense sun and harsh elements, creating an environment where children and adults can meet to share music, drama and ideas. Constructed from disused military parachutes, the pavilion is a fitting reminder of the intrusion of war on everyday lives, yet also highlights the positives which can emerge from conflict. The BaSiC initiative collaborated with local pupils and Buddhist nuns to reimagine the parachutes, stitching them into a tensile structure which resolves structural and design issues, while also symbolising the peace and unity the school and community hope for.

MEDIA-TIC BUILDING
BARCELONA

ENRIC RUIZ-GELI // CLOUD 9

☆ Nominated by LUCY BULLIVANT: "All Enric Ruiz-Geli's buildings are very advanced ecologically and you can read that ambition in their appearance. Media-TIC, in the emerging 22@BCN science and technology district of Barcelona, 'performs' its energy efficiency through a membrane of pneumatic cushions, which activate the solar energy regulation on its facade. This is the first use of the versatile hybrid material ETFE within Spain. Dubbed 'the digital Pedrera', the building is a hub for information technology businesses with an affinity for Antoni Gaudi's interest in nature as geometry. Media-TIC is about the performance of nature, how it creates physical change and produces clean energy, light and warmth. With an 80 per cent suspended steel-frame structure, the architecture teaches us something. Media-TIC is 'muy emblemático': the first green building of the green city Barcelona wants to be." — LB

ruiz-geli.com
e-cloud9.com

IMAGE © LUIS ROS AND CLOUD 9

Taking inspiration from sources as diverse as quilts and jellyfish, Media-TIC is a mixed-use office building with public galleries. The latest contribution to Barcelona's science and technology district, the structure itself is packed with innovative technology. Its facades inflate or deflate according to the strength of the sun, making it one of the most energy-efficient buildings in Spain. Cushioned layers of ethylene tetrafluoroethylene (ETFE) – a material similar to that used in geodesic domes such as Cornwall's Eden Project – are injected with nitrogen-based fog, which allows the desired amount of light and heat into the building. Structurally, the building is based around a huge load-bearing exoskeleton, or superstructure, from which all the floors are suspended. This unorthodox approach to construction provides expansive wide floors undisturbed by columns or other structural elements.

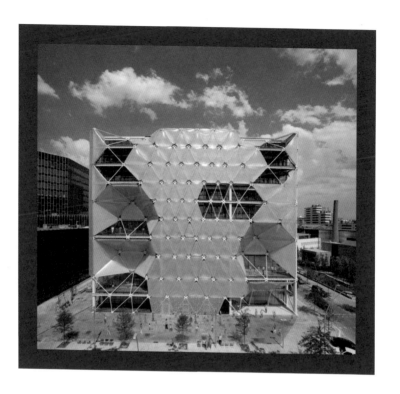

NOTTINGHAM CONTEMPORARY
NOTTINGHAM

CARUSO ST JOHN ARCHITECTS
Client: NOTTINGHAM CITY COUNCIL

☆ Nominated by RAYMUND RYAN: "Nottingham Contemporary's varied galleries enrich the art-viewing experience by drawing connections to the city while also reintegrating the unorthodox site into the historic grain of the area. The galleries alter in size and height, typically illuminated from above, with occasional windows for lateral views. The project brings pattern back as a topic for serious architectural research, with exterior concrete panels reproducing a sample of Nottingham lace as ornament. The entire project is a bespoke tailoring of programming requirements, topography, urban linkages and iconography. This intelligent fusion provides a model for middle-sized institutions across Europe." — RR

carusostjohn.com

IMAGE © HELENE BINET

The design for Nottingham Contemporary draws inspiration from Nottingham's heritage in contemporary art, performance and object-based work, and directly engages with the city site. Caruso St John offer a wide selection of interiors with the variety and specificity of found spaces. These flexible areas provide public yards, cinemas, theatres and galleries alongside commercial and education zones. The exterior is inspired by local nineteenth-century architecture and, in particular, by the impressive facades of the Lace Market, where hard brick forms a robust shell around the repetitive structural frames of warehouse buildings. Nottingham Contemporary's facades present a continuous patterned surface of pale green pre-cast concrete elements. The pattern is taken from a specific example of Nottingham lace, which was scanned, modified and then converted into a three-dimensional mould.

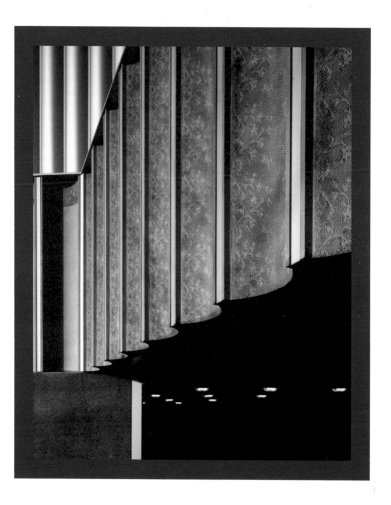

OPEN AIR LIBRARY
MAGDEBURG

KARO ARCHITEKTEN
Participation process: ARCHITEKTUR+NETZWERK
Client: LANDESHAUPTSTADT MAGDEBURG

☆ Nominated by HUIB VAN DE WERF: "In a former East-German post-industrial city with 80 per cent vacancy an initiative to bring residents together was called for. This community project, launched in collaboration with the citizens of Magdeburg, allowed residents to create the Open Air Library themselves. No registration is required to check out books. You simply take one and return it within a reasonable amount of time, or bring back a different old book. The project not only added a patch of green space to the industrial city, it also established a community-oriented institution based on the trust of neighbours." — HVDW

karo-architekten.de

IMAGE © ANJA SCHLAMANN

The development of the Open Air Library began five years ago with a public intervention on the fallow site of a former public library. Once a 1:1 model of a possible new open air library was constructed from beer crates, the empty bookshelves rapidly filled up with donations from the community. Inspired by the project, local residents campaigned for many years to raise the money needed to construct a permanent facility. As a reference to the former industrial nature of the district, the library's facade is constructed from panels reclaimed from the exterior of a nearby 1960s modernist warehouse. KARO designed the library as an outdoor space where the bookshelves are never closed and you can take a book whenever you want. With no bureaucracy, the library runs on trust.

STONEBRIDGE HILLSIDE HUB
GREATER LONDON

EDWARD CULLINAN ARCHITECTS
Client: HYDE HOUSING ASSOCIATION // HILLSIDE ACTION TRUST

☆ Nominated by WAYNE HEMINGWAY MBE: "When I moved to London in 1979, I rented a cheap place in Wembley. Ever thrifty, the future Mrs H and I walked the six miles home along the Harrow Road from nights out at Le Beat Route and Club for Heroes. A mile from home we would 'leg it' past the notorious Stonebridge Estate as fast as our little legs could carry us; even the postmen and milkmen refused to enter this crime-ridden and depressing carbuncle. In later years I cycled through the estate on the way to meetings, always a little wary. Today it is one of the best examples of how intelligent design can make a place liveable and uplifting. This is transformational design at its very best: a world class project." — WH MBE

edwardcullinanarchitects.com

IIMAGE © EDMUND SUMNER

Stonebridge Hillside Hub is a mixed-use landmark building forming the final phase of a 14 year regeneration of the troubled Stonebridge Estate. The project unites separate community facilities within one single building, with the overlapping functions allowing each element to serve, and be served by, the others. The result is a financially and socially self-sustaining development. Two wings contain mixed-tenure residential apartments, a primary care centre, café and convenience store. The strongly articulated central section includes a community centre, with a public piazza at the front and a private landscaped garden behind. The building is designed so visitors can clearly identify individual elements. Apartments are clad in Siberian larch, the primary care centre uses high quality white brick with coloured panels and a zinc roof forms a graceful curve over the community centre.

TAPE INSTALLATIONS

NUMEN/FOR USE

☆ Nominated by THOMAS GEISLER: "This temporary architecture made from ordinary sticky tape invites people to experience space in a new way. Reminiscent of experimental and avant-garde architecture, such as Frederick Kiesler's Endless House, the structure explores the possibilities of habitation, using industrial material in a completely different mode. Still in an experimental stage, the project could lead to new ways of constructing cocoon-like structures." — TG

foruse.eu

IMAGE © NUMEN/FOR USE

Between 2009 and 2010 the Croatian–Austrian collective Numen/For Use created a number of site-specific installations from rolls of sticky tape. Multiple layers of transparent tape act like tendons stretched between rigid points and columns. The continuous wrapping of these links results in complex, amorphous shapes reminiscent of growing organic forms. Days of work and 45km of tape went into creating some of the structures, which can be experienced from inside as well as out. It is the introduction of the audience inside the structures that transforms them from sculpture into architecture. The concept originated from a set design for a dance performance, in which the form evolves from the movement of dancers between pillars: the dancers stretch the tape as they move, resulting in a (tape) recording of the choreography.

UK PAVILION SHANGHAI EXPO 2010

HEATHERWICK STUDIO

☆ Nominated by PAOLA ANTONELLI // SHANE WALTER: "An outstanding demonstration of Britain's design and architecture innovation, delivered with poise and poetry. Whether it's bridges, buildings or products, Heatherwick deals in the extraordinary. His UK Pavilion is a delight, a beguiling work of art constructed from 60,000 acrylic tendrils, each containing a seed from Kew Gardens' Millennium Seed Bank. Its optic filaments gently quiver in the breeze, creating an effect likened to dandelions and sea urchins. These shafts draw light into the pavilion during the day and direct it outwards at night. With the sadness that the building won't stay intact, comes the knowledge that the rods and seeds will be distributed to Chinese and UK schools after the expo — carrying this magical masterpiece much, much further in the minds of tomorrow." — SW

heatherwick.com

IMAGE © IWAN BAAN

In 2007 Heatherwick Studio won the competition to design the UK Pavilion for the Shanghai 2010 Expo. Responding to the event theme of Better City, Better Life, the pavilion was made of two interlinked and experiential elements: the Seed Cathedral and a multi-layered landscape treatment exploring the particularity of nature and UK cities. The Seed Cathedral highlighted the work of the Royal Botanic Gardens, Kew and their Millennium Seed Bank. The 20m high building was constructed from thousands of 7.5m long transparent optical strands, each with a seed embedded within its tip. The interior was silent and illuminated only by daylight filtering past each seed and optical hair. Just as dandelion seeds blow away and disperse on the breeze, the Seed Cathedral's 60,000 strands, each containing the potential for life, will now be distributed to hundreds of schools across China and the UK.

UNIVERSITY OF OXFORD: DEPARTMENT OF EARTH SCIENCES

WILKINSON EYRE ARCHITECTS
Client: UNIVERSITY OF OXFORD

☆ Nominated by JAMES DYSON: "Oxford is dominated by bulky buildings with unknown purposes. It's a challenge for the city to put up buildings that acknowledge its people as well as the university. Wilkinson Eyre's design opens up what happens inside the building, featuring an exterior wall that will be updated with ideas generated in the Department of Earth Sciences. Good design and engineering communicates something about the way a product or building functions. And people like to know what happens inside." — JD

wilkinsoneyre.com

IMAGE © MORLEY VON STERNBERG

The University of Oxford's Department of Earth Sciences is designed to meet the academic requirements of the department and also to signal to the wider public the interests and concerns of those working within it. The building works as a 'found' object, telling the story of its users in the same way a fossil communicates about a particular geological era. This concept is embodied in the 'narrative wall', the building's most striking element, which acts as a shop front for the department. Internally, the building includes a laboratory wing and office zone, with an atrium 'hinge' joining the two. The ground floor contains undergraduate common areas, a library, lecture theatre and display space. The senior common room is located on the top floor, with views over Oxford and a roof terrace. This position is seen as important for encouraging interaction and interdisciplinary exchange of ideas.

VITRAHAUS
WEIL AM RHINE

HERZOG & DE MEURON
Client: VITRA VERWALTUNGS GMBH

☆ Nominated by DAVID ROWAN: "VitraHaus in Weil am Rhein, Germany, by Swiss architects Herzog & de Meuron, is an extraordinarily inspiring structure. A showcase for the Vitra Collection at the Vitra Campus — alongside structures by architects such as Frank Gehry and Zaha Hadid — it consists of a dozen stacked 'houses' and, from a distance, looks like a precarious pile of buildings. Inside, the space serves as a clean, if angular, display setting for Vitra furniture. At night, the windows glow and welcome the gaze of passers-by. Brilliant and original." — DR

vitra.com/en-un/campus/vitrahaus/

IMAGE © IWAN BAAN

VitraHaus is a showroom for furniture manufacturer Vitra's wide-ranging product portfolio and associated collection. The displayed objects are designed primarily for the private home and are therefore not presented in the neutral atmosphere of a conventional hall or museum, but rather in an environment suited to their character and use. VitraHaus uses a direct, architectural rendition of a basic house form, which is stacked and extruded to create complex configurations merging outside and inside spaces. The interior is designed with surprising transitions between rooms and views of the exterior landscape. The idyllic Tüllinger Hills, the broad expanse of railroad tracks, and the urbanised plane of the Rhine can all be viewed from the glazed gable end sections of each level.

VOID HOUSE
BRUSSELS

GON ZIFRONI in collaboration with POM-ARCHI

☆ Nominated by HUIB VAN DER WERF: "Aside from the architect's immaculate taste for hyper-modernism and minimal aesthetic, the Void House also serves a practical purpose for its surrounding community. The void on the ground floor beneath it allows public access to the back garden during the day, which therefore becomes public property. It is exemplary that something so individual as a private residence can also contribute selflessly to its surroundings." — HVDW

pom-archi.com

IMAGE © FILIP DUJARDIN

The Void House is Brussels-based designer Gon Zifroni's first completed building. A family house, it takes its name from the large ground level void which provides wide, flowing access to the garden below and beyond. By removing the ground floor entirely the void beneath is directly accessible from the street and becomes a semi-public space. Internally, a series of open rooms are arranged around a central staircase, creating a sensation that the entire volume of the house is viewable from any point within. The finish is extremely minimal, constructed from a limited pallet of materials which includes aluminium and brushed metal. Wood panelling used for walls and floors is constructed from natural bamboo slats processed without treatments or toxic adhesives.

FASHION

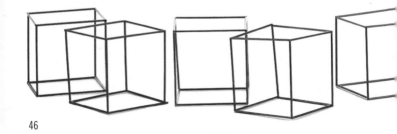

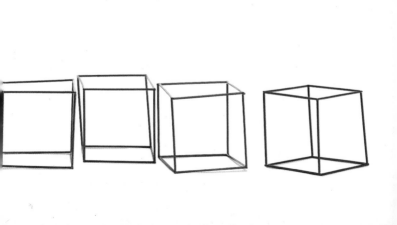

COMME DES GARCONS TRADING MUSEUM
TOKYO

Designed and conceived by REI KAWAKUBO

☆ Nominated by ALISON MOLONEY: "Rei Kawakubo and her team at Comme des Garçons have continually pushed the boundaries of retail innovation, most notably as the protagonists of the pop-up shop revolution. Last year they expanded their ground-breaking retail empire with the introduction of the Comme des Garçons Trading Museum. Situated within the Gyre Building, a shopping centre in Tokyo designed by Dutch architects MVRDV, the Trading Museum is part shop and part exhibition space. Antique display cases have been replicated or transformed to create curiosity cabinets containing vintage Comme des Garçons pieces alongside its new collection and a selection of work by emerging and established designers. This fusing of culture and commerce acknowledges the role of window shoppers who may be unable to afford the clothes, but still become brand-advocates." — AM

doverstreetmarket.com

IMAGE © COMME DES GARCONS

Comme des Garçons have always striven for innovation in every aspect of their brand. Following on from guerilla pop-up stores in the early 2000s and the London Dover Street Market store, Rei Kawakubo's Trading Museum in Tokyo continues the trend. Designed and conceived by Kawakubo, the museum is based around a series of vintage display cabinets bought from the V&A. The cases contain a careful mix of retail and more traditional museum content. Some display items to buy, others objects to view. Some showcase garments, others magazines and perfumes. Some of the content is vintage, the rest brand new. The past year has seen content as varied as Comme des Garçons' take on The Beatles, Stephen Jones's hats and punk T-shirts. It is this studious combination of elements that makes the Trading Museum such a success.

GARETH PUGH
SPRING/SUMMER '11

Designed by GARETH PUGH

☆ Nominated by SONNET STANFILL: "In September 2010, Gareth Pugh showed his Spring/Summer '11 collection of appealing and thought-through ensembles. Pugh's reputation for creations that are part theatre, part fantasy connects him to London's long tradition of fashion experiment and iconoclastic design vision. With this important collection Pugh has created softer, wearable ensembles that retain the designer's tendency toward the fantastical: tunics of silvery armour, garments with a scale-like construction and bold, sculptural silhouettes. Pugh continues to explore unusual fabrics such as rubberised neoprene and nylon printed with aluminium." — SS

garethpugh.net

IMAGE © GARETH PUGH

Featuring high necklines, tight-tailoring and a futuristic Samurai aesthetic, Gareth Pugh's Spring/Summer '11 collection displayed a softness unseen in his previous work. Fabrics such as silicone-coated jersey on a neoprene base were moulded around the body, creating unexpectedly refined silhouettes which explode into slashed trousers or shorts. Aluminium-coated nylon acted as a two way mirror and super reflective silver, slashed by hand, delivered a modern take on camouflage. Shunning the traditional catwalk presentation, Pugh is the latest example of a young fashion designer employing new ways to make his designs more widely accessible. During Paris Fashion Week he exhibited his collection by showing a film directed by Ruth Hogben, and featuring supermodel Kristen McMenamy, in the Parc de Bercy sports stadium.

LANVIN
SPRING/SUMMER '11

Designed by ALBER ELBAZ

☆ Nominated by PAULA REED: "Alber Elbaz has turned the label Jeanne Lanvin founded in 1889 into one of the most wanted of the twenty-first century. Recognised for his technical skill and innate sense of what women want to wear, Alber compares French high fashion to the culture of a cordon bleu kitchen. While he respects the techniques, he acts like a chef working without double cream. The result is modern clothing stripped of fussy structure, decoration and weight. Lanvin may be the oldest French fashion house but, with Alber Elbaz at the helm, it is also one of the most modern. Alber has managed the well nigh impossible task of staying true to a 130 year heritage while setting the pace for contemporary fashion." — PR

lanvin.com

IMAGE © LANVIN

Lanvin's Spring/Summer '11 collection kicked off with combinations of flowing feminine dresses and wide belts, each accenting the waist and emphasising the body. Full-length dresses gave way to elegant businesswear which, in turn, morphed into evening dresses. Though the bright neon colours of these cocktail dresses were sharp and unmistakable, the structure of the designs and the appreciation of the often ruched fabric were never lost. The collection culminated in a series of sophisticated looks incorporating metallic and tribal prints. It was the variety of pieces that was most impressive, with ideas of choice and adaption central to the collection's development. Despite influences from past designers, Alber Elbaz's work is always connected to the present. As he himself says, 'to be relevant, clothes have to be related to the time we live in'.

MARGARET HOWELL PLUS SHIRT

Designed by KENNETH GRANGE // MARGARET HOWELL

☆ Nominated by JAMES DYSON: "This is how a shirt should be constructed, with every part carefully considered. It is not designed to draw attention to itself, or to the wearer. It simply does the job. No fussy collar – just clean, practical lines and a comfortable fit. Kenneth Grange came up with a wonderful granite pen holder for desks and his shirt does the same with a different material, as the layered pocket is the right size and shape to carry pens and pencils. Margaret Howell is a great advocate of British design talent. What an interesting way to express this!" — JD

margarethowell.co.uk

IMAGE © MARGARET HOWELL

Plus is a series of collaborations between Margaret Howell and designers from other fields, whose work she particularly admires. The first shirt in the range is designed in partnership with Kenneth Grange, the British industrial designer responsible for Parker Pens and InterCity Trains. The result is a unique shirt reflecting the external design input as well as the premium quality associated with Margaret Howell. The Plus Shirt is collarless, with a generous fit and minimal styling. It features a button-fly front and a unique pocket designed for pens. Grange selected a classic slate-grey cotton fabric with a paler grey on the inner collar band and cuffs. Each shirt is made by a single machinist in Howell's London workshop. The fine quality cotton is supplied by Thomas Mason, the label's first and continuing supplier of material.

MELONIA SHOE

Designed by NAIM JOSEFI // SOUZAN YOUSSOUF

☆ Nominated by ED ANNINK: "Naim Josefi and Souzan Youssouf, of Beckmans and Konstfack respectively, designed and modelled the shoes for selective laser sintering (the one with all the powder and the lasers) and produced five pairs for Naim's Melonia collection. What an exciting idea to design your own shoe, a product in which many things come together: function, comfort, status and symbolism. I guess a designer and a software navigator are needed to lead the process…" — EA

beckmans.se/naim-josefi

IMAGE © NAIM JOSEFI

The Melonia Shoe is a collaboration between fashion designer Naim Josefi and industrial designer Souzan Youssouf. As a counterpart to Josefi's 2010 Melonia collection the designer produced a design for an accompanying shoe, which Youssouf rendered in three-dimensional software. A rapid-prototyping process was then used to 'print' the shoes. As a new vision for shoe production, the software has been developed so that customers may visit a shop where their foot is scanned, and an individual, personally-tailored pair of shoes can be produced. The shoes are the first 3D-printed haute couture shoes in the world and were inspired by the ecologic concept of 'no material waste'. The homogeneous nylon material is easy to recycle, creating a closed manufacturing and disposal loop.

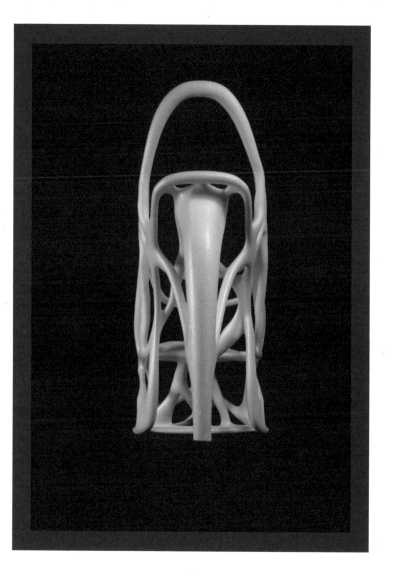

OHNE TITEL
SPRING/SUMMER '11

Designed by FLORA GILL // ALEXA ADAMS

☆ Nominated by PAOLA ANTONELLI: "It all started with a coup de foudre in Spring/Summer '08, but with the unforgettable Spring/Summer '11 show we all knew Ohne Titel was here to stay. Even without knowledge of their excellent apprenticeship with Karl Lagerfeld and their collaborations with artists — Tauba Auerbach featured this season — Alexa Adams and Flora Gill's garments are feats of design and manufacture that enhance a woman's body with punk grace and well-constructed comfort." — PA

ohnetitel.com

IMAGE © OHNE TITEL

Ohne Titel's public and commercial standing has soared in recent years. Yet this jump in sales and status has not lessened the label's appeal with the arty fashion scene that has followed the young designers since they started out. For the Spring '11 collection, designers Alexa Adams and Flora Gill took inspiration from the prints of Japanese artist Utagawa Kuniyoshi. Adapting linear shapes, colour blocking and open volumes into a modern silhouette, they experimented with striated sheer cottons combined with slick neoprene. The graphic palette comprised white, navy, cobalt and black, with touches of fluorescent yellow and red. A swimsuit feel was central to many of the looks and continued the suggestion of athleticism present in much of the designers' previous work. Accessories included geometric tubular necklaces, developed in collaboration with artist Tauba Auerbach.

ORGANIC JEWELLERY COLLECTION

Designed by FLAVIA AMADEU

☆ Nominated by ADELIA BORGES: "The rubber sheets are produced by micro latex processing plants installed in the Brazilian Amazon and operated by local rubber tappers and their families. This Tecbor technology was developed by the Chemical Technology Laboratory at the University of Brasilia, and enables the preparation of pre-coloured sheets. The innovative design takes advantage of the flexibility and lightness of the material, with bracelets and necklaces becoming three-dimensional when placed on the body. It is a good example of how design can empower forest inhabitants and workers, contributing value without devastation." — AB

flaviaamadeu.com

IMAGE © FLAVIA AMADEU

Flavia Amadeu's Organic Jewellery Collection is made from an eco-friendly rubber known as Tecbor (Technology for the production of rubber and artefacts in the Amazon). Originating from natural latex, Tecbor is produced by native communities in the Amazon rainforest. The efficient, semi-industrial, production process generates minimal waste and improves the properties of the natural rubber. Consequently, the quality of life of the local communities is also improved. Amadeu exploits Tecbor's natural characteristics, such as elasticity, malleability, resistance and colour, to add aesthetic value. Her flat, one-size, jewellery pieces fit many different body shapes, transforming into three dimensions when worn.

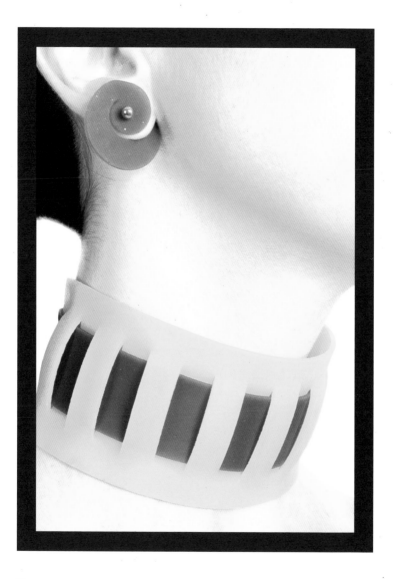

TESS GIBERSON SPRING/SUMMER '11, SHIFT

Designed by TESS GIBERSON

☆ Nominated by SONNET STANFILL: "After a hiatus of several years, during which she served as lead designer for the TSE cashmere label, New York-based Giberson has reinstated her eponymous clothing line. Relaunched with Autumn/Winter '10-11, Giberson furthered her reputation for thoughtful, poetic collections designed around a central theme. The Spring/Summer '11 collection, titled Shift, was shown in September 2010. Giberson avoids the pendulum changes and inherent waste of the fashion cycle with ensembles that are quiet but considered. Shift includes asymmetric shirtdresses, double-layered tank dresses and the occasional tailored jacket. These garments are Giberson's solution for the simple urban wardrobe." — SS

tessgiberson.com

IMAGE © AMY TROOST

Tess Giberson's Shift collection examined the many meanings of the title word. In both subtle and exaggerated form, shift is explored by transferring details, rearranging materials and repositioning the balance of a garment. Vests are turned upside down to create skirts, pockets are moved from one garment to another, the structured front of a jacket is replaced with fine mesh and the back panel of another jacket is removed entirely. The collection was presented as a multimedia installation incorporating clothing, objects, video and music. Giberson collaborated with artist Carol Bove to arrange clothing, found and fabricated objects throughout the space. An Alia Raza video was also presented, featuring actress Elodie Bouchez, musician Sadie Laska and stylist Jessica de Ruiter: three strong creative women embodying the character of the collection.

UNIQLO +J
AUTUMN/WINTER '10

Designed by JIL SANDER for UNIQLO

☆ Nominated by PAULA REED: "The brand manifesto says it all: 'luxury will be simplicity; purity in design, beauty and comfort for all; quality for the people'. As designer of her eponymous collection, Jil Sander was recognised for impeccably tailored clothes at impossibly expensive (for most people) prices. Collaboration with a fast fashion outlet therefore seemed an unlikely possibility. But her collection for Japanese high street chain Uniqlo set a new standard for accessible luxury. The collection excelled at delivering Sander's intention to bring quality basics to the masses – not always the result when high-end designers create lines for mass chains. Being able to buy a well-made, good-fitting, Jil Sander-designed winter coat for £130 is arguably a sign of the times, but certainly, in the business of luxury fashion design, pretty revolutionary." — PR

uniqlo.com/plusj

IMAGE © UNIQLO

Jil Sander's initial collaboration with Uniqlo gained worldwide recognition from both the high-end fashion world and the high street. While this latest collection has evolved since the collaboration's inception a year ago, the designs continue to explore the territory between couture and sportswear. Emphasising the silhouette, easy and gracious movement, practicality and the perfect fit, +J is characterised by pure tailoring and avant-garde textiles. Arctic blues, tempestuous greys and warm foliage colours are complemented with fine wools, cashmere, flannel and beautiful felt coats. A new edition of the widely acclaimed +J white shirt exudes subdued sophistication. Spun from luxurious Egyptian cotton, well fitted and sculptured, this one item encapsulates Sander's objective of creating key wardrobe pieces, which work seamlessly with almost anything else.

FURNITURE

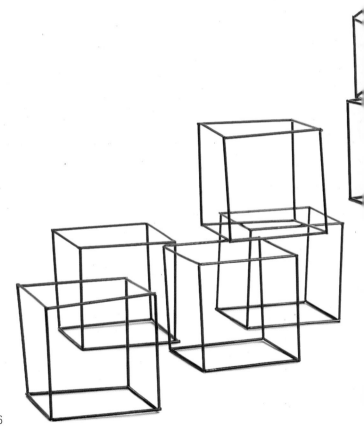

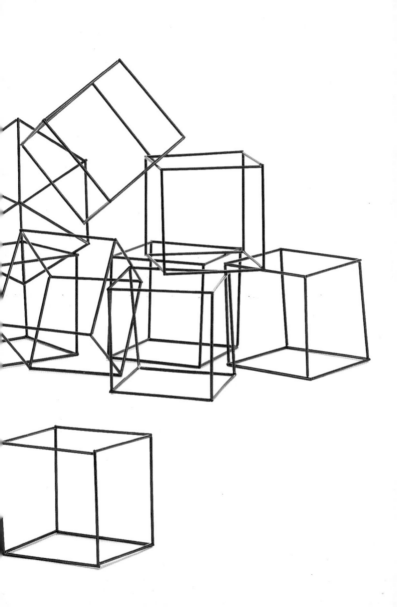

BRANCA

Designed by INDUSTRIAL FACILITY // SAM HECHT //
KIM COLIN // IPPEI MATSUMOTO
Manufactured by MATTIAZZI

☆ Nominated by DANIEL CHARNY: "Though it might look just like an elegant bentwood chair, Branca is part of the latest revolution in the fantastic story of wood carving. A skill as revered as it is derided may now find a renewed lease of life through a combination of robotic and handcrafted processes. The complexity of the three-dimensional design is most evident in the way the armrest grows out of the back leg, which is made of one strong part. Inspired by the unique skills of the computerised cutting robot operator, and drawing from the seductive growth structures of tree branches, Industrial Facility's chair may yet prove to be a celebrated case in the pursuit of industrial quality growing out of craft knowledge." — DC

industrialfacility.co.uk
mattiazzi.eu

IMAGE © INDUSTRIAL FACILITY

The Branca chair is familiar to the eye, its design drawing on the concept of the growth of trees. Like branches supporting the joints of twigs and leaves, Branca's back legs support the critical joints of the armrest, seat and back, all made from a single piece of wood, which is produced robotically. The joints are but a part of the seamless nature of the chair and its simple outline belies the complexity of its production. Branca offers all the functional attributes we expect in a modern chair: to be comfortable, to have armrests, to fit under a table, to be light enough to carry and to stack for easy shipping.

COLLEC+ORS COLLECTION

Designed by KHAI LIEW // JULIE BLYFIELD // KIRSTEN COELHO // JESSICA LOUGHLIN // BRUCE NUSKE // GWYN HANSSEN PIGOTT // PRUE VENABLES

☆ Nominated by BRIAN PARKES: "Khai Liew, who has always worked with skilled artisans in producing his furniture, was one of a select number of Australian designers and makers to exhibit at the annual Collect decorative arts fair in London from 2004 to 2008. Shared sensibilities were identified among these exhibitors and friendships grew, with Liew instigating a series of collaborations that explore these aesthetic and personal relationships. In August 2010 Liew launched this group of six bespoke furniture pieces in Adelaide, South Australia. The history, utility and humility of furniture became the language of collaborative dialogue between Liew and ceramic artists Kirsten Coelho, Gwyn Hanssen Pigott, Bruce Nuske and Prue Venables, glass artist Jessica Loughlin and silversmith Julie Blyfield. The resulting pieces combine like choral voices to pay moving homage to the relationship between design and craftsmanship." — BP

khailiewdesign.com

IMAGE © KHAI LIEW

Collec+ors is a collaborative and interrelated body of works initiated by Khai Liew. Six pre-eminent Australian visual artists were invited to make work illustrative of their current practice, which would then be integrated within an individual, one-off design by Liew. The idea being that the sum of the parts is greater than the single object; the communal effort is as important as the individual pursuit. Collectively there is a shared aesthetic vision, a common language underpinned by overlapping frames of reference, a rigorousness of process and meticulous attention to detail.

DROP TABLE

Designed by JUNYA ISHIGAMI
Manufactured by LIVING DIVANI

☆ Nominated by FRANCESCA PICCHI: "In this collaboration with an established furniture company, Junya Ishigami exploits manufacturing processes to create something close to a one off: a transparent table with a transparent top which acts as an optical device like a kind of magnifying lens. The entire production process takes over 50 hours, including rough-hewing, finishing operations and smoothing and polishing by hand. Light distortion through the tortuous path of the complex curved surface seems to go beyond the simple concept of transparency. Objects on top not only appear to float in the air, they seem to be swallowed up into a parallel dimension. Manufacturers Living Divani say the table 'distorts the perception of space and changes the distances between objects like a mirage'." — FP

livingdivani.it

IMAGE © TOMMASO SARTORI FOR LIVING DIVANI

Available as both a low coffee table and dining table, Drop is envisaged as a sculptural object that both represents and distorts space. Created from a single piece of perspex, the lower part of the table top is curved like a lens, playfully manipulating the perceived sense of depth beneath. Like a mirage, the distance between objects is vague, causing those arranged on the surface to blend and produce a harmonious, even image. The production of Drop involves computer-controlled techniques to create the table top and three individually shaped legs. In addition, labour-intensive finishing procedures (using abrasive paste, polishing wax and finishing polish) are all performed by hand. The resulting optical effect is the combination of a craftsman-like approach to design and a sophisticated industrial manufacturing process.

DUNE

Designed by RAINER MUTSCH
Manufactured by ETERNIT

☆ Nominated by THOMAS GEISLER: "A modular multi-configuration outdoor lounge made for public spaces. Constructed from the same material as Willy Guhl's beautiful classic, Dune offers a new interpretation of the Loop Chair. Its sculptural nature gives a more pleasant appearance in urban or suburban environments than many similar products. Maybe it will even calm down potential vandals – or at least provide a challenge for their creativity." — TG

rainermutsch.net
eternit.at

IMAGE © RAIMUND APPEL

Designed as modular furniture for public spaces and outdoor use, Dune is an expandable system with an endless number of combinations. The shape of all five elements allows the user to freely move on the objects and choose an individual seating position. This flexibility guarantees maximum comfort and, when the elements are arranged in a group, multiple opportunities for communication. Due to its modularity Dune not only fits all spatial situations, it also creates spaces on its own. The additional integration of plants generates extra textures and shadows and allows further customisation. Manufactured from fully recyclable fibre-cement panels, which consist of 100 per cent natural materials such as cellulose fibres and water, the units are durable and able to withstand the demands placed on public seating.

ENDLESS

Designed by DIRK VANDER KOOIJ

☆ Nominated by ED ANNINK: "By combining different techniques, Dirk vander Kooij, a 2010 graduate of the Design Academy Eindhoven, was able to design an automated but very flexible process. He taught an old robot to produce a chair out of scrap plastic — an endless strip of plastic used to make endless variations in product types, colours and shapes. A robot as craftsman, designer and curious researcher. Plastic scrap as material. And, by the way, the chair is very comfortable too!" — EA

dirkvanderkooij.nl

IMAGE © DIRK VANDER KOOIJ

Endless is a chair constructed from recycled refrigerators, extruded by a programmed robot in a single continuous ribbon. The unusual production technique is in a sense itself recycled. Design Academy Eindhoven graduate Dirk vander Kooij rescued his robot from a Chinese production line after a 140,000 hour non-stop career and transformed it into a large-scale prototyping machine. For each chair the production process requires the designer to work in tandem with the robot, rendering the practice a combination of traditional craft techniques and industrialised production. Avoiding the inflexibility of modern automated production, Endless allows vander Kooij to design in a more 'old-fashioned' way: making a chair, evaluating and refining it, making a chair, evaluating and refining it, making a chair and so on.

ORIGIN PART I: JOIN

Designed by BCXSY in collaboration with MR TANAKA

☆ Nominated by HENRIETTA THOMPSON: "Unveiled at Spazio Rossana Orlandi, this series of three dividing screens was widely appreciated as one of the most elegantly realised designs at Salone del Mobile. Join brought elegant contemporary design together with tategu, the art of Japanese wood joinery. In each piece two lined frames – a familiar form in tategu – are visually merged to create a new aesthetic. The angles and shapes introduced in the intersection diverge from the traditional process, and required some dedication and perseverance on the part of the tategu craftsman. As designers Boaz Cohen and Sayaka Yamamoto learned during this project: there is a reason for every step, a story behind every pattern. They describe the main challenge as 'developing a project that was innovative yet still honoured traditional aspects of the craft'." — HT

bcxsy.com

IMAGE © BCXSY

Join is a series of three space dividers handmade by Mr Tanaka, a master craftsman in traditional Japanese wood joinery (known as tategu). In each piece two lined frames, representing the humble integrity inherent to the craft, are visually merged to create a product which departs from the conventional tategu aesthetic. The intention is to respect the traditional core of the technique while raising awareness and interest for the vanishing craft. Join screens are entirely handcrafted from hinoki wood (Japanese cypress), with the exception of the brass hinges. The wood is highly rot-resistant and traditionally used untreated, historically for the making of bathtubs. The tategu technique allows the joining of material through highly precise joints, with minimal glue and no screws or nails.

PLYTUBE

Designed by SEONGYONG LEE

☆ Nominated by HENRIETTA THOMPSON // GARETH WILLIAMS // JANE WITHERS: "Seongyong Lee has successfully developed an entirely new material with myriad applications for furniture and larger scale architectural applications. His Plytubes are made like ubiquitous cardboard tubes, but instead of laminating sheets of paper, he has used sheets of wood veneer. This increases the tubes' strength and durability while also enhancing their sensuous, silken quality. He has made his early prototypes entirely by hand. What is needed is an imaginative manufacturer to take the project to the next level. By adapting an existing archetype, he has added great value to it." — GW

seongyonglee.com

IMAGE © SEONGYONG LEE

Plytube is a new material manufactured by applying the technologies for making basic cardboard tubes to veneer wood. Recent Royal College of Art graduate Seongyong Lee's process wraps laminates together and hardens them with glue. Created from a minimal amount of material Plytubes are very light, extremely strong and suitable for many different types of tooling and finishes. The resulting series of furniture demonstrates the specialist qualities of Plytube, including structural rigidity, lightness, the aesthetic quality of joints and finishes, and hollowness as a function.

SAYL TASK CHAIR

Designed by YVES BEHAR // FUSEPROJECT
Manufactured by HERMAN MILLER

☆ Nominated by SAM HECHT: "Designer Charles Eames would often say Herman Miller had the ability to create 'the best, to the most, for the least'. In office seating they have never lost this vision. Their history is littered with visionary advances in ergonomics and innovation. This latest endeavour uses a plastic moulded mesh, stretched like fabric to form the chair back. The structure gives lightness and comfort, and makes it the most affordable task chair Herman Miller has ever created." — SH

fuseproject.com/products-60
hermanmiller.com

IMAGE © FUSEPROJECT

The SAYL chair is the lowest cost task chair Herman Miller has ever produced. SAYL combines ergonomics, material savings, quality, aesthetics and comfort. One of the main distinguishing elements is its full-suspension frameless back. Different degrees of tension are infused directly into the injection-moulded material, providing sacral, lumbar, and upper spine support, and the three-dimensional intelligence of the design lets the chair adapt to an individual's shape and movements, providing constant support. Removing unnecessary elements resulted in the development of the Y-shaped rear tower and the ArcSpan, which allows fine-tuning to mirror spine curvature. As with other recent Herman Miller chairs the SAYL is cradle-to-cradle certified. While essentially eco-driven, the certification process is critical for both functional ergonomics and design aesthetic.

SOLO BENCH

Designed by DOMINGOS TOTORA

☆ Nominated by ADELIA BORGES: "Discarded cardboard and empty bags of cement are mixed with water and glue to create a material with the resistance and behaviour of wood. The material and the resulting pieces of furniture, objects and sculptures are handmade by local craftsmen trained by Domingos. This project is a good example of the initiatives that have recently taken place in Brazil, which promote craftsmanship to generate income for underprivileged populations, while also respecting the environment. It has social and environmental dimensions, which, in my view, should be key issues when evaluating contemporary design." — AB

domingostorora.com

IMAGE © DOMINGOS TOTORA

Solo Bench is part of Domingos Tótora's line of recycled cardboard furniture. After studying design in São Paulo, Tótora returned to his hometown, Maria da Fe, in the mountainous region of Minas Gerais, where the local landscape and a passion for nature serve as inspiration for his work. Motivated by the huge amount of material discarded by local businesses, the designer began to use cardboard as a source material. Starting with recycled cardboard pulp he creates objects and sculptures where beauty is inseparable from function, granting an artistic aura to common everyday objects. Tótora trains local craftsmen in certified sustainable processes to construct furniture which falls between art and design.

SPUN

Designed by HEATHERWICK STUDIO
Manufactured by MAGIS

☆ Nominated by DANIEL CHARNY // DAVID ROWAN:
"Metal spinning is a way of forming flat sheets into
symmetric shells over a mould. It is a surprising and
ancient craft that creates magical moments similar
to watching clay transform on a potter's wheel.
Spun's appearance captures this sense of surprise
visually, but also when you sit down and lean back
into the seat and succeed in making a full spin. It is
a refreshing design and a new typology for a rocking
seat. This is apparent in the successful translation
of the design from the luxury of the collector's
gallery into a technology enabling access for a larger
audience. It is also satisfying to see how knowledge
of a type of making inspired an idea, which made
its way into a new and delightful design." — DC

heatherwick.com

A completely rotational
symmetrical form, Spun grew
out of Heatherwick Studio's
research into simplifying
the geometry of an object
as familiar as a chair. Using
full-size test pieces, a seating
ergonomic was developed
where the seat, back and arms
all share the same profile.
The result is not immediately
recognisable as a chair. When
upright it looks more like a
sculptural vessel. On its side,
however, it forms a comfortable
and functional chair, in which
the sitter can rock from side
to side or even spin round
in a complete circle. Spun is
made using rotational plastic
moulding, an efficient and low
cost manufacturing process
which involves heating plastic
pellets in a spinning four-part
mould to form a uniform-
thickness wall. The process
also enables a rippled surface
texture to be imparted into the
piece, accentuating its form.

THIN BLACK LINES

Designed by NENDO
Exhibited by PHILLIPS DE PURY & COMPANY
at THE SAATCHI GALLERY, LONDON

☆ Nominated by CAROLINE ROUX // HENRIETTA THOMPSON: "Nendo, a seven-strong Tokyo design team led by Oki Sato, has long been the one to watch in Japan. This year's Thin Black Lines lived up to all expectations of their work, which relies on an economy of means and unique sense of invention, rather than aesthetic or formal style. The furniture pieces all appear to have been drawn in the air, sharing the character of Japanese calligraphy to produce objects which are simultaneously two- and three-dimensional. They both suggest furniture archetypes and exist as pieces themselves – representational and fully functional at the same time. The pleasure they give comes from all these things, compounded by exquisite workmanship. The illusion of these objects cutting through space is only sustained by their flawless finish." — CR

nendo.jp
phillipsdepury.com

IMAGE © MASAYUKI HAYASHI

The Thin Black Lines series includes furniture, lamps and vases exploring the theme of outlines. The series was developed in cooperation with Phillips de Pury & Company and first exhibited in their Saatchi Gallery space during the 2010 London Design Festival. Rendered in simple black lines fashioned from bent steel, the forms are inspired by Japanese calligraphy. The distinct graphic quality allows playful manipulation of perspective, with objects often appearing as two-dimensional shapes and three-dimensional forms simultaneously. As your eye traces slight black lines outlining the pieces, volumes and surfaces appear and disappear, and the practical function of the product comes into focus.

VIGNA CHAIR

Designed by MARTINO GAMPER
Manufactured by MAGIS

☆ Nominated by FRANCESCA PICCHI: "Known for an actionist approach to design, Martino Gamper focuses his efforts on real action executed in real time. The Vigna chair is one of his first projects to involve mass production with an established company. Asked to use welded metal wire, he developed a continuous form of chair, drawing inspiration from a growing vine plant. Like a climbing stem, the thin metal wire curls up to form the elegant shape of the chair." — FP

gampermartino.com
magisdesign.com

IMAGE © MAGIS

With his first design for Italian furniture manufacturers Magis, Martino Gamper took inspiration from one of the most popular examples of early mass manufacturing, the ubiquitous Thonet bentwood chair. Keen to avoid a superficial postmodern reimagining, the legs of the Vigna chair climb like vines – from which the chair gets its name – entwined around one another to form the main structure on which the seat is fixed. In another clever reference, Vigna's seat element is made using double-injection plastic moulding, a favoured industrial process of contemporary mass-manufactured furniture. This mimics Thonet's revolutionary use of steam-bent wood for mass production. The combination of a steel rod frame and plastic seat allows Vigna to be produced in any two colours.

GRAPHICS

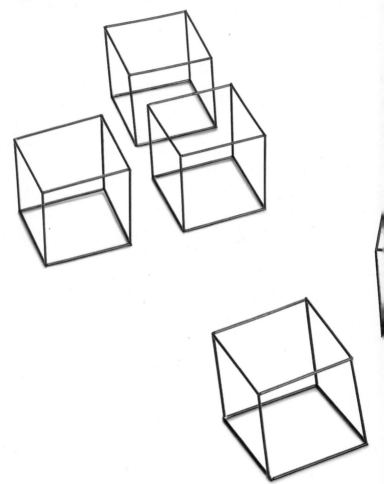

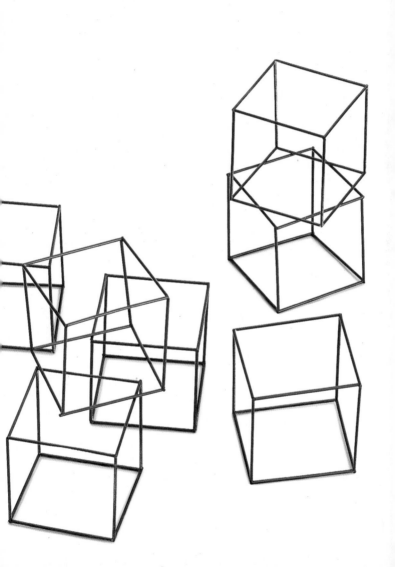

A LOVE LETTER FOR YOU

Designed by STEPHEN POWERS // ICY // THE MURAL ARTS PROGRAM // THE PEW CENTER FOR ARTS AND HERITAGE

☆ Nominated by ALEX BEC: "The A Love Letter For You project reaffirms your faith in humanity. In a world of funding cuts, technological advances and material desires, Stephen Powers plainly reminds us what it means to be human. The ease of communication in his trademark mural painting is something to be admired and, although seemingly straightforward, the eloquence of execution confirms Powers as an undoubted master of the art. We are entering a time when all but the essentials risk being axed from our cultural landscape. If nothing else, we can take inspiration from initiatives like the City of Philadelphia Mural Arts Program, built to support such projects. This is the one project I fell in love with in 2010 and I challenge you not to be equally woo-ed." — AB

aloveletterforyou.com
muralarts.org

IMAGE © STEPHEN POWERS

As a member of the Inner City Youth (ICY) graffiti club in the 1980s Stephen Powers spent many hours clambering over rooftops to paint his tag, ESPO. 25 years later he returned home to West Philadelphia to organise an unprecedented community arts project. In consultation with the local community, businesses and property owners, a series of murals containing hopeful messages were painted across rooftops spread along an elevated train route. The resulting love letter, meant for one but with meaning for all, encompasses 50 walls facing the Market–Frankford train line. Using 1200 cans of spray paint, 800 gallons of bucket paint and the skilled hands of the finest spray painters in America, Powers' wanted to create a single, serial urban work that would resonate with a neighbourhood in need of hope.

COALITION OF THE WILLING

Direction and production by KNIFE PARTY
Written by TIM RAYNER
Voiceover artist: COLIN TIERNEY

☆ Nominated by SHANE WALTER: "Coalition of the Willing is an animated film about an online war against global warming in a post-Copenhagen world. Under the helm of Simon Robson this was an ambitious 'swarm' project from the start. Content aside, the novel multi-collaborative production approach and serial dissemination marked it as one to watch. The finished work is also beautifully crafted, galvanising a network of 24 artists from around the world using moving image techniques to perfectly support the aim. The film was released in sections every two to three weeks, via a bespoke website over a six month period. This unconventional release strategy allowed audiences to build and become engaged during production and beyond. The culmination of this work is a coherent, well-made, provocative, and engaging accomplishment." — SW

coalitionofthewilling.org.uk
knife-party.net
timrayner.net

IMAGE © KNIFE PARTY

Coalition of the Willing is a collaborative animated film dedicated to galvanising the world's public in the fight against global warming. Written in the immediate aftermath of the 2009 Copenhagen Climate Summit, the initial animator, Simon Robson, soon realised his chosen in-camera animation route would take forever to complete. He then invited a network of artists from around the world to collaborate, using varied and eclectic techniques. The intense 14 month production period involved 17 animation units and 78 individuals creating 30 different sections. The finished film is an optimistic exploration of the use of new internet technologies to leverage the power of activists, experts and ordinary citizens in collaborative ventures. Through analyses of swarm activity and social revolution, the film explains how to hand the climate change fight to the people, as a new online activism.

DESIGN CRIMINALS EDIBLE CATALOGUE

Designed by ANDREAS POHANCENIK

☆ Nominated by THOMAS GEISLER: "The Design Criminals exhibition, curated by Sam Jacob/Fat at MAK Design Space, brought together a bunch of emerging Austrian designers to contribute to the Loosian discourse on 'ornament and crime' by working with everyday decorative arts. Contemporary cake decoration and graphic design share the same ingredients and tools: a printer and ink. By collaborating with a chef de cuisine, Andreas Pohancenik made a catalogue from completely edible materials. Simultaneously solid and ephemeral, it questions how we keep records of our digital time, while also representing Vienna at its best: pastry!"
— TG

practiceandtheory.co.uk

IMAGE © ANDREAS POHANCENIK

Produced as a catalogue to accompany Sam Jacob's Design Criminals exhibition at the Vienna MAK, this 'consumable book' is entirely edible. Its typographic slipcase is made of pastillage, a technique which involves the shaping of sugar. Individual pages are made from wafer printed with coloured vegetable ink. Some of the books were created on site at the MAK with visitor involvement. Attendees at an evening event were then invited to eat the printed wafer pages and pastillage ornaments. Although overthrowing the usual function of a catalogue, Andreas Pohancenik's work supported the exhibition's subversive theme, as the perishable and sweet-tasting product encouraged visitors to participate in its destruction.

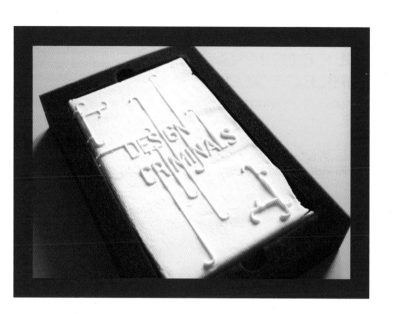

FOUR CORNERS FAMILIARS SERIES

Designed by JOHN MORGAN STUDIO and collaborators

☆ Nominated by CATHERINE INCE: "Vanity Fair is the latest – and lushest – volume in the Familiars series. In artist Donald Urquhart's inky, graphic illustrations Bette Davis is cast as heroine Becky Sharpe, lending a sassy twentieth-century feel to Thackeray's classic. Set in the girlishly named Felicity and Perpetua typefaces, and wrapped in a sweet, pale-pink dust-jacket with matching pink headbands and ribbon bookmarks, this edition heaves with saccharine femininity. Accessibly priced yet fiendishly collectible, each Familiars book is a 'print re-enactment' – a subtle re-assessment of an old or 'lost' text. John Morgan's starting point is a meticulous exploration of the work's first published edition, its textual characteristics or the historic social and cultural context. The carefully conceived approach to each design combined with the collaborating artists' illustrations and printer Martin Lee's beautiful production never fails to seduce." — CI

fourcornersbooks.co.uk/familiars
morganstudio.co.uk

IMAGE © JOHN MORGAN STUDIO

Four Corners Familiars series features artists' responses to classic novels and short stories, providing a fresh look at the tradition of the illustrated novel. Artists, generally without experience of illustrating text, are approached to choose a favourite novel and then commissioned to create new work printed alongside the existing text. Contributors are encouraged to interpret 'illustration' as loosely as they wish, and to suggest new ways in which texts and images can relate to one another. The result is magazine adverts appearing in The Picture of Dorian Gray, images of 1930s Hollywood within Vanity Fair and text illustrating text in Nau Sea Sea Sick. Unusually for a series, the designed form of each individual book responds to the needs and atmosphere of the title-specific artwork and text.

HOMEMADE IS BEST

Designed by FORSMAN & BODENFORS for IKEA

☆ Nominated by DAVID KESTER: "One of the many fantastic interactive graphic campaigns which caught our attention this year was the work done by Forsman & Bodenfors, as part of the agency's 15 year relationship with multinational retailer IKEA. The Homemade is Best cookery book and iPhone app show how designers can captivate new customers with creative, smart and fun campaigns, using interactive media as well as beautifully designed print." — DK

demo.fb.se

IMAGE © CARL KLEINER // AGENT BAUER

Faced with developing an IKEA marketing campaign, Forsman & Bodenfors soon realised the best way to get people excited about microwave ovens, fridges and fans is to talk about the delicious things you can make with them. As a hub for a whole marketing campaign, Homemade is Best is a 140 page baking book of classic Swedish recipes, presented in spectacular visual style. The recipes are depicted as warm and colourful graphic still-life portraits, with all the ingredients laid out in carefully arranged and composed photographs. Inspired by high fashion and Japanese minimalism, the concept for the book moved the cakes and finished products into the background and put the ingredients centre stage.

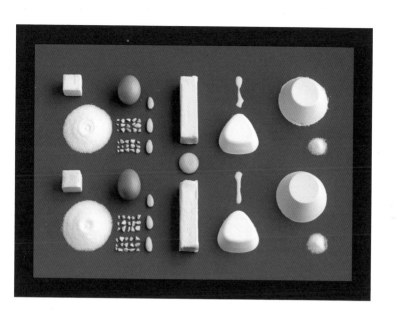

IRMA BOOM:
BIOGRAPHY IN BOOKS

Designed by IRMA BOOM
Published by GRAFSICHE CULTUURSTICHTING

☆ Nominated by PAOLA ANTONELLI: "Clients,
whether curators, designers, or companies in need
of a strong design catharsis, know that hiring Irma
Boom will get them a deeper, better, truer self-portrait
in an unforgettable book. But can she be her own
client? Faced with the need to condense her oeuvre
for a museum retrospective, the biggest and most
self-effacing book designer in the world has churned
out the smallest 'catalogue raisonné'." — PA

grafischecultuur.nl
irmaboom.nl

IMAGE © IRMA BOOM

This miniature book contains
a complete overview of Irma
Boom's work, presenting over
450 full-colour illustrations
in 704 pages. Boom is one
of the world's most widely
renowned book designers and,
in a refreshing antidote to
the usual coffee table design
books, her biography of work
to date measures just 5cm
high. The inspiration for the
tiny tome is a reflection of the
process Boom herself uses
when designing. Known for
making tiny models of all her
books, often creating six or
seven of each, Boom uses them
as filters for ideas and tools
to help the book's structure
evolve. Irma Boom: Biography
in Books was designed for
the designer's retrospective
exhibition at the Special
Collections of the University
of Amsterdam Library. It
includes text by Mathieu
Lommen and notes by Boom.

I WONDER

Written, illustrated and designed by MARIAN BANTJES
Published by THAMES & HUDSON

☆ Nominated by SIMON ESTERSON: "We all know print is having a hard time, so it's a pleasure when someone comes along and loudly reaffirms the virtues of the book. And this isn't just a nice design job: Marian Bantjes wrote the text and the design of each chapter springs from its content. Reworkings of traditional manuscript forms, page designs constructed from pasta, flow diagrams about assembling IKEA bookshelves: they're all here in Marian's unique combination of the drawn and the digital. I Wonder is visually rich, physically tactile and beautifully produced. Credit should also go to Bantjes' publisher, Thames & Hudson, for backing I Wonder and doing it properly, right down to the gilded page edges." — SE

bantjes.com/i-wonder

IMAGE © MARIAN BANTJES

Marian Bantjes' densely decorated book is designed to be a treat for both the senses and the mind. The cover is hardbound with a black satin finish, foil stamped on front and back in gold and silver. With gilded page edges, the book looks and feels like a block of gold. Inside, the ornamented pages examine the role of wonder in design, using imagery and thoughtful, funny and quirky writings. The author, illustrator and designer's writing is accessible and at times teasing, inspiring the reader to contemplate the world in an unorthodox way and fostering leaps of the imagination when looking at everyday things. Reminiscent of illuminated manuscripts, the graphics echo the text's eclectic appearance and makeup, mixing historically evocative forms with contemporary materials – from gold patterning to displays involving cereal, jewellery, tinfoil, and macaroni.

LONDON COLLEGE OF COMMUNICATION POWER OF TEN SUMMER SHOW '10

Designed by MORAG MYERSCOUGH

☆ Nominated by IAN CARTLIDGE: "This is a great example of how the graphic concept for a fundamental necessity (navigating a space) can transform and revitalise a whole building. Studio Myerscough's signage does much more than make the LCC building navigable. It influences how students think and feel about their environment, surprising and delighting in a way which was surely unanticipated by the client. This is immediately evident externally, where the LCC have successfully created a street presence on the brutal Elephant and Castle roundabout. By populating the small triangular space outside the main entrance with brightly-coloured shipping containers, which function as galleries, tables, chairs and even a cappuccino van, Studio Myerscough has created an unexpected, vibrant and social space in an extremely challenging environment." — IC

studiomyerscough.com

IMAGE © AIDAN BROWN

Over recent years Morag Myerscough/Studio Myerscough has brought to life the indistinct internal architecture of the London College of Communication (LCC). The work reflects LCC's typographic, print and design heritage as well as the distinctive tactile and expressive qualities of the specialist studio-based education taking place within the building. The latest phase of the project transformed the triangular 'piazza' outside the college. Shipping container galleries, carnivalesque spaces and colourful seating areas delivered a permeable extension to the college's internal activities. This external placemaking and wayfinding successfully bridged the gap between the college and its uncompromising urban location. It is the first step towards a new image and identity for the college, and promotes a sense of pride in community as the local area regenerates.

THE LIFE AND OPINIONS OF TRISTRAM SHANDY, GENTLEMAN

Designed by A PRACTICE FOR EVERYDAY LIFE
Written by LAURENCE STERNE
Published by VISUAL EDITIONS

☆ Nominated by SIMON ESTERSON // WILL HUDSON: "The Life and Opinions of Tristram Shandy, Gentleman is a masterstroke of twenty-first-century publishing. In an era where digital platforms take centre stage, Visual Editions are flying in the face of adversity. Having only recently set out their stall, it looks like Anna and Britt are onto something really rather special. An absolute pleasure to read, Visual Editions have brought together elements that fit seamlessly together: a notable author, a great story, plus the fantastic designers at A Practice For Everyday Life who added visual elements that complement the ethos behind visual writing. Most importantly, Anna and Britt contribute optimism and excitement about why we should still print, and read, books." — WH

apracticeforeverydaylife.com
visual-editions.com

IMAGE © VISUAL EDITIONS

When Visual Editions briefed designers A Practice For Everyday Life (APFEL) to look into the history of the 129 published editions of The Life and Opinions of Tristram Shandy, Gentleman, they discussed breathing new life into the book's original humour and maverick spirit. In the 1759 two-volume first edition, Laurence Sterne subverted the available print and typographic techniques to illustrate points in his loquacious and semi-autobiographical tale of daily life. As an initial research project, APFEL worked through this first edition highlighting each of Sterne's interventions — from the use of different length dashes and asterisks, denoting words too rude to print, to pages printed entirely in black or marble effect. For this new edition, these visual interventions have been reimagined, creating a publication where the visual elements are not decorative or extraneous, but inseparable from the text itself.

UNIT EDITIONS

Designed by TONY BROOK // ADRIAN SHAUGHNESSY

☆ Nominated by JEREMY LESLIE: "A new publishing imprint launched by designer Tony Brook and design critic Adrian Shaughnessy that circumvents the usual marketing/distribution model, providing a design-led curatorial voice across a new series of publications. Distributed via their website (and a few selected book stores), published projects include books about designers' workspaces, a newspaper about punk single sleeve design and limited edition posters. A breath of fresh air for the design publishing world." — JL

uniteditions.com

IMAGE © UNIT EDITIONS

Unit Editions is a new, progressive publishing venture producing high-quality, affordable books on graphic design and visual culture. A collaboration between self-confessed book lovers, Tony Brook and Adrian Shaughnessy, Unit Editions combines impeccable design and production standards with insightful texts and informative commentaries on a wide range of subjects. Publications have included three editions of Unit: Design/Research (a series of papers devoted to graphic design and visual culture), Studio Culture (a glimpse into the inner workings of 28 leading graphic design studios) and Supergraphics (chronicling the early days of a 1960s and 1970s architectural movement). Although Unit Editions produces books 'for graphic designers by graphic designers', it makes them accessible to anyone with even a passing interest.

Unit: Design/Research 01   *Ronald Clyne at Folkways*

Unit: Design/Research 02   *Space and structure*

Unit: Design/Research 03   *ThreeSix*

Editors:
Tony Brook
Adrian Shaughnessy   Unit 02

INTERACTIVE

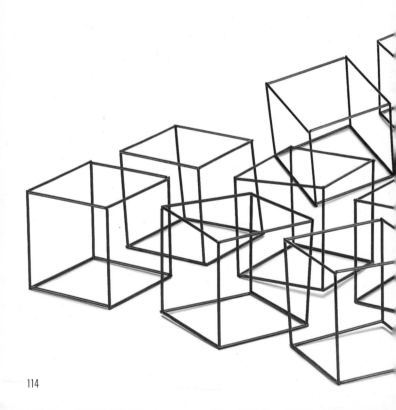

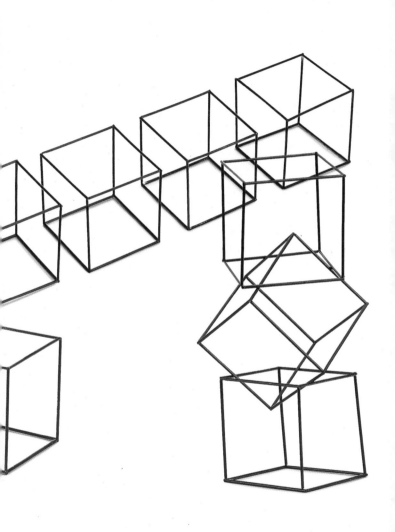

ANGRY BIRDS

Designed and developed by ROVIO MOBILE

☆ Nominated by MATT JONES: "You're on public transport in London, Chicago or Shanghai. Glance around you, and it's likely there's someone playing Angry Birds. Created by Rovio, a small Finnish games design house, with a budget a fraction of most console game development costs, Angry Birds dominates the downtime of commuters worldwide. It's a simple game — you catapult the titular angry birds toward their enemies (smug looking pigs) and delight (or dismay) in blowing down their ramshackle houses. It's spawned cuddly toys, an advertising and payment mechanism, even a feature film is in development. The 'Chuck Jones' appearance might not be the most elegant, but this is digital toy-making at its best. In terms of global attention commanded by a design, it can't be beaten in 2010." — MJ

rovio.com

IMAGE © ROVIO

Angry Birds is a multi-platform mobile game which has generated global communities, live action events and a range of related merchandising. The game itself is remarkably simple, an essential requirement for something designed to be played in short bursts by almost anyone. Launching flightless birds at the houses of egg-stealing pigs, hits on critical weak points bring down houses and earn points. Angry Birds' success lies in its intuitive simulation of real world physics and the ease with which players understand the flight trajectory of the airborne birds and the structural properties of the buildings under attack. Development took eight months, with a core team of four developers. By the end of 2010, Angry Birds had been downloaded over 50 million times across various platforms, making it one of the most popular mobile games ever created.

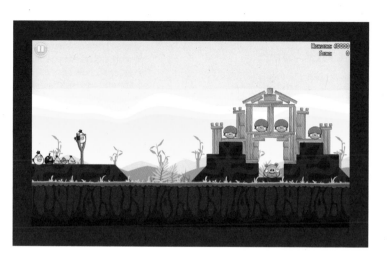

CELLSCOPE

Designed by DANIEL FLETCHER // THE CELLSCOPE TEAM
Animation by AARDMAN ANIMATIONS
Animation commissioned by WIEDEN+KENNEDY
for NOKIA

☆ Nominated by DAVID KESTER: "CellScope combines a mobile (cell)phone and a microscope lens. Invented by scientist Daniel Fletcher and developed in collaboration with designers and creative professionals, it can be used to diagnose diseases such as malaria, in remote locations with limited access to hospitals. With a fairytale film story about a tiny girl, Aardman Animations has demonstrated the detail a CellScope can capture. The film is a fantastic example of how collaboration between designers, creative professionals, scientists and technologists can generate exciting new concepts with real social and economic value. 'It's not the technology, it's what you do with it,' says the team itself. Congratulations to them all." — DK

aardman.com
cellscope.berkeley.edu
wk.com

IMAGE © MICHAEL ROSENBLUTH

CellScope uses mobile phone-enabled telemicroscopy to link patients with doctors no matter where they are in the world. The CellScope team have developed an automated, compact, and portable system capable of image capture, image processing and communication with medical experts. The approach could dramatically improve access to basic healthcare, enabling patients to be active participants in their own care and allowing doctors to customise drugs and dosing based on real-time feedback. Inspired by CellScope, Aardman Animations created the world's smallest stop-motion animation film, following a 9mm-tall character as she runs through an obstacle course made of currency, rides a bumblebee, and stitches her way out of trouble.

E.CHROMI

Designed by ALEXANDRA DAISY GINSBERG // JAMES KING, in collaboration with CAMBRIDGE UNIVERSITY'S IGEM TEAM

☆ Nominated by PAOLA ANTONELLI: "Design is much more than making chairs or posters. We all know that. But a diagnostic tool based on engineered bacteria that colour one's faeces to highlight the presence of different diseases? Designers like Ginsberg and King allow both scientists and laypeople to access and understand complex ideas and systems. Their collaboration with scientists won iGEM, the unique showdown amongst synthetic biology teams from all over the world, held yearly at MIT in Cambridge, Massachusetts." — PA

daisyginsberg.com
echromi.com
james-king.net

IMAGE © ALEXANDRA DAISY GINSBERG & JAMES KING // OSA JOHANNESSON

E.chromi is a novel collaboration between designers and scientists in the emerging field of synthetic biology. Seven University of Cambridge undergraduates recently took the Grand Prize at the International Genetically Engineered Machine competition (iGEM), for designing E.coli bacteria that can secrete colours visible to the naked eye. They named this new variety E.chromi. Designers Alexandra Daisy Ginsberg and James King worked with the team, exploring the potential of the technology as it was being designed. Together they designed a timeline for how this foundational technology might affect our lives over the next century. From printing inks and food colours to disease monitoring and pollution mapping, these future scenarios are not always desirable, but they explore the different agendas that could shape the use of E.chromi and, in turn, our everyday lives.

FLIPBOARD

Designed by MIKE McCUE // EVAN DOLL

☆ Nominated by PATRICK BURGOYNE // JEREMY LESLIE: "One of the lessons of the internet is that some of the most successful ideas have been based on the principle of aggregating and organising what is already out there and presenting it in a useful and appropriate way. A huge amount of money has been thrown at creating magazine apps but Flipboard leapfrogs the old-fashioned thinking that has mired such endeavours, to deliver a personalised, constantly updated information source entirely fitting for its medium." — PB

"The most exciting attempt to date at connecting the visual possibilities presented by the iPad with the sharing potential of social networks. Digital content from Twitter and Facebook is algorithmically designed into 'pages' using images and text from links contained in tweets and posts. A first but highly important step towards engaging digital content on the iPad." — JL

flipboard.com

IMAGE © FLIPBOARD

Flipboard has been conceived as the world's first social magazine. Inspired by the beauty and ease of print media, Flipboard aims to fundamentally improve how people discover, view and share content across social networks. Readers create their own sections based on content from Facebook, Twitter, Flickr and Google Reader and quickly flip through the latest stories, photos and updates from friends and trusted sources. The single magazine-style format means readers no longer have to scan long lists of posts and click on link after link. Instead they instantly see all their stories, comments and images, making it faster and more entertaining to discover, view and share social content. Since July 2010, when Flipboard launched as a free iPad app, the project has received recognition and praise across the design, web and publishing industries.

hello

GUARDIAN EYEWITNESS iPAD APP

Designed by THE GUARDIAN TECHNOLOGY TEAM (ANDY BROCKIE // ALASTAIR DENT // JONATHAN MOORE // MARTIN REDINGTON // ROGER TOOTH)

☆ Nominated by SIMON ESTERSON: "In the midst of the storm that is newspaper publishing, the Guardian plotted a smart course when it came to the launch of the iPad. Rather than trying to offer an app that did everything, they chose to concentrate on doing one thing exceptionally well. Eyewitness takes the double-page spread news pictures run in the centre of the printed paper and offers them as a downloadable gallery which is updated daily. If you touch the screen the captions disappear and the picture fills the frame. Eyewitness plays to the Guardian's strong tradition of picture editing and the iPad's amazing screen quality and intuitive touchscreen actions. When other newspapers went tabloid, the Guardian waited, thought and went Berliner. Now we wait for the full Guardian iPad app…" — SE

guardian.co.uk/ipad

IMAGE © GUARDIAN

Selected by Apple as one of the apps to showcase iPad to the world, Eyewitness offers access to some of the most distinctive and provocative photographs. Developed by the Guardian, it has been downloaded by nearly 500,000 iPad users worldwide and is widely regarded as one of the most successful apps to date. Eyewitness provides free access to the Guardian's award-winning photography series and is devoted entirely to showcasing the best photos in superb detail, allowing users to fully appreciate the work the photographer has put into each and every image. Features include technical insights from award-winning photographers, and the ability to save photos as favourites and share them via email, Twitter and Facebook.

INTERACTIVE: UK

MIMOSA

Designed by JASON BRUGES STUDIO for PHILIPS

☆ Nominated by SARAH WEIR: "A mix of creative flair and artistry, interactive developing technology and technical expertise are all apparent in Jason Bruges Studio's Mimosa, which shows this mix at its very potent best. By turn intelligent, thought-provoking, playful, seductive, innovative and fun, Mimosa brings together cutting-edge technology, great beauty and sensitivity to the organic forms of plants. Watching people's response to this piece was fascinating. No instructions were necessary. It drew an entirely instinctive reaction and was a source of great amusement, puzzlement and intrigue. This is always a hallmark of Jason's work and in my view is what makes it so successful." — SW

jasonbruges.com

IMAGE © JASON BRUGES STUDIO

Philips commissioned Jason Bruges Studio to create an artwork for the 2010 Salone del Mobile as a showcase for the organic LED (OLED) technology developed at their Lumiblade Creative Lab. Mimosa is an interactive artwork consisting of slim OLED panels arranged in petal configurations to form flowers. A motion sensor mounted above reacts to movement from nearby people, opening and closing the delicate petals and changing the light conditions. The piece was inspired by the mimosa family of plants, which open and close in response to environmental conditions. OLED technology is relatively new in consumer-facing products. It creates light by passing electricity through one or more extremely thin layers of organic semiconductor material.

PAINT

Designed by GREYWORLD for NOKIA

☆ Nominated by DALJIT SINGH: "Users place a paint bucket in a filling station and watch their image flow into it. They then throw their painted face over the wall, watching dripping paint flow across the surface to reveal the faces of previous players. Participants can also use phones to 'throw paint', by blowing on, flicking or swiping the screen. Paint employed the basic rules of interactivity and delivered them brilliantly; picking up a bucket is a familiar and natural action. This type of interaction should involve surprise and delight. Paint did this by the bucket load!" — DS

greyworld.org/archives/572

IMAGE © GREYWORLD

Paint is an installation commissioned by Nokia to mark the launch of their new N8 phone. London-based art and design studio Greyworld developed the installation, which substitutes paint for pixels. Participants pick up an empty paint bucket and place it in a nearby column, which acts as a virtual filling station. A camera at the top of the column takes a quick photo of the user, and this picture is used to 'fill up' the bucket. Players then 'throw' their painted face all over the nearby wall, without ever handling any real paint. The installation used an LED wall, motion sensors and an acute understanding of how people intuitively interact with objects.

REACTABLE MOBILE

Designed by REACTABLE SYSTEMS

☆ Nominated by DEE HALLIGAN: "Miniaturising the original Reactable and adapting it for touch screen (which meant eliminating the tangible interface – really the unique element of the original) makes no sense on paper. The resultant product interface looks great, echoing the original as you might expect, but the changes are more fundamental. Being mobile, it changes how you access it and where it's available. Casual use makes mastering the interface seem less critical and consequently the possibility of mastering it becomes more available. The physical original implies a performance; the app gives you permission to goof around and geek out, alone. And the price widens the market to include skill-less idlers like me. The tangible interface may follow, but the mobile product stands perfectly well on its own, without reference to any original." — DH

reactable.com/products/mobile

IMAGE © REACTABLE SYSTEMS

Reactable first attracted the world's attention in 2007 and 2008, when Icelandic musician Björk toured the world with a strange, bright and hypnotic new instrument. Developed by the Music Technology Group at Pompeu Fabra University in Barcelona, Reactable is a circular, table-top musical instrument. The translucent acrylic pucks can be manipulated, combined and interconnected by one or more musicians. This creates challenging and immediate ways to control different components of a modular synthesiser. Reactable Mobile is a more accessible model, available as a downloadable app on a variety of platforms. The software combines the original concepts of modular synthesisers (sampling, digital audio effects and DJ-ing) with multi-touch technologies to provide access to this intuitive music creation experience for anyone with a touch screen device.

ROCK BAND 3

Designed by HARMONIX MUSIC SYSTEMS

☆ Nominated by ROSS PHILLIPS: "The latest iteration of the popular Rock Band franchise includes support for keyboards and a range of features that further streamline the experience, but its real innovation lies in further bridging the gap between playing the game and playing a real instrument. With pro mode, users can learn how to play the actual instruments of a real band, encouraged along by tutorials, achievements and leaderboards. Added to an already accomplished mix proven to be an enduring multiplayer (both local and online) favourite, this is the definitive version of Rock Band and the pinnacle of the interactive music genre." — RP

harmonixmusic.com/#games
rockband.com

IMAGE © MAD CATZ

Earlier incarnations of Rock Band allowed people to live out their rock 'n' roll fantasies in the privacy of their own home. Using instrument-shaped game controllers, players mimed along to classic and modern rock soundtracks, on their own or with friends. The latest version makes some important advances. With innovative game modes and controllers, and new and improved instruments, Rock Band 3 changes the way users think about and play music games. The addition of a pro mode and realistic instruments, including full drum kits, keyboards and guitars styled like Fender Stratocasters, has delivered a level of gameplay so realistic that the experience moves from pure entertainment to an educational interaction. Genuine instruments with MIDI capabilities can also be connected and used to control the game.

SPEED OF LIGHT

Designed by UNITED VISUAL ARTISTS
Commissioned by VIRGIN MEDIA

☆ Nominated by PATRICK BURGOYNE: "I generally approach anything involving lasers with the extreme caution of one who has been disappointed by far too many 'spectacular' light shows over the years, but Speed of Light was different. As a promotional stunt for Virgin, it was both novel and exciting. As an installation in its own right it was spectacular, thrilling even." — PB

uva.co.uk/archives/126
vminstore.com/speedoflight

IMAGE © UNITED VISUAL ARTISTS

Speed of Light is a series of installations exploring themes of communication and modernity. Commissioned by Virgin Media to mark the tenth anniversary of UK broadband with an immersive light experience, United Visual Artists stripped fibre optics back to their minimum: thin strands of glass and flickering beams of light. Dramatising the experience of fibre-optic communication, the installation transforms an input from the audience into a pathway of light, which leads through the atmospheric exhibition environment. The continuous beam of light evolves through each installation in turn, shifting in intensity and form. Speed of Light used over 100 lasers across four floors and six rooms of the Bargehouse, a raw and industrial warehouse on the South Bank.

THE ELEMENTS
iPAD APP

Designed by TOUCH PRESS
Written by THEODORE GRAY

☆ Nominated by PATRICK BURGOYNE: "One of the few editorial iPad apps that offers a genuinely engaging experience tailored to the medium. The interactive elements are beautifully realised in a very rewarding piece of content that both informs and delights." — PB

periodictable.com/ipad
touchpress.com

IMAGE © TOUCH PRESS LLP

The Elements: A Visual Exploration is the first complete e-book developed from the ground up for iPad. Expanding on the hardcover coffee table book of the same name, the interactive app starts as a living periodic table where every element is represented by a smoothly rotating sample. To read about tin, tap on the tin soldier. To read about gold, tap on the gold nugget. Immediately, users see a sample of the element filling most of the large screen, photographed with razor sharpness and rotating through 360 degrees. Beautifully imaged objects, and samples representing the element, then fall into place. Every item is a freely rotatable, live object, which can be examined from all sides. Some pages also offer video experiments or stereo three-dimensional images viewable with 3D glasses.

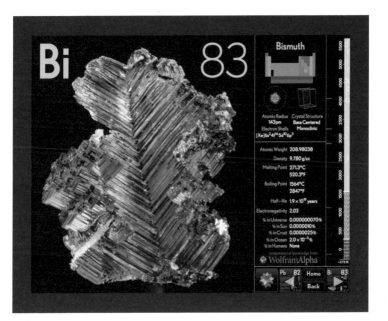

THE JOHNNY CASH PROJECT

Designed by CHRIS MILK // AARON KOBLIN // RADICAL MEDIA // RICK RUBIN // THE CASH ESTATE

☆ Nominated by SHANE WALTER: "Another stand out project collaboration between Milk and Koblin. User-generated content driven by crowdsourcing and swarm engagement for a global, online, self-perpetuating viral campaign, The Johnny Cash Project can handle more new media buzz than a fresh copy of Wired. What truly makes this stand out is the pure emotion and humanity that comes through thousands of people each drawing over a single video frame to create a series of personal portraits of Johnny Cash. Played in sequence over Ain't No Grave, Cash's final studio recording, this is a fitting, moving homage to this beloved musician, ultimately delivering a unique visual testament to how the 'man in black' lives on and continues to inspire. As the creators say 'Thank you for helping Johnny's spirit soar once more'." — SW

thejohnnycashproject.com

IMAGE © THE JOHNNY CASH PROJECT 2010

The Johnny Cash Project is a communal artwork, creating a living portrait of the musician known as the 'man in black'. Working with a single image template, and using an embedded custom drawing tool, participants create a unique and personal portrait of musician Johnny Cash. Their work is then combined with art from around the world, and integrated into a collective whole: a crowd-sourced music video for Ain't No Grave rising from a sea of one-of-a-kind portraits. Strung together and played in sequence over the song, the individual handmade portraits create a moving, ever evolving homage to Cash. As new people discover and contribute to the project, the living portrait continues to transform and grow, and it is virtually never the same video twice.

WALLPAPER* CUSTOM COVERS

Art Direction by MEIRION PRITCHARD
Interaction design and programming by KIN
Content by ANTHONY BURRILL // HORT // JAMES JOYCE
// NIGEL ROBINSON // KAM TANG

☆ Nominated by PATRICK BURGOYNE // SHANE WALTER: "The challenge: a mighty 20,000 unique, handcrafted magazine covers, all created by subscribers. A near impossible project – sure to deliver average results at best – was turned into a triumph by the hands and heads of new media thinking, Kin. Like all great ideas, their application appeared cheekily simple on the surface but surely used a huge amount of production and creative grey matter behind the scenes. Kin brilliantly made the whole process collaborative and open, inviting designers to create assets for their system before letting it be 'played with' by thousands of the reading public. A huge, collaborative, tour de force bundle of superb digital craft, exemplary production endeavour, adventurous client, smart thinking, and high creative goals." — SW

kin-design.com
wallpaper.com/custom-covers

IMAGE © WALLPAPER* // KIN DESIGN

The Custom Covers project enabled anyone to design and receive their own individual cover for the August 2010 edition of Wallpaper* magazine. Using state-of-the-art digital printing and military-precision planning, 21,000 unique covers were printed on seven different paper stocks and delivered to subscribers. The user-facing online design application used pre-designed elements, icons and graphics, which were then converted into high resolution files. Even subscribers who didn't design a cover still received a unique design, developed by a program which randomised these elements. Once printed the covers were bound on a traditional binding line and distributed worldwide through Wallpaper*'s usual channels.

WIRED MAGAZINE iPAD APP

Designed and developed by SCOTT DADICH // JEREMY CLARK // CONDE NAST DIGITAL

☆ Nominated by SIMON ESTERSON: "2010 was the year of the iPad, and the boom industry of third-party apps sold through Apple's iTunes store. The early video demo of Wired's online magazine (for a device that was yet to be announced) was a revelation to print designers and publishers. To designers it showed an online design that wasn't a website. To publishers it showed you could publish online and charge for it. Scott Dadich, Wired's Creative Director, and his team were already making one of the best art-directed print magazines in the world and when their app appeared it was clear they had brought the same thinking to the new device. There will be second thoughts and other ways of doing things, but the Wired app is a pioneer of this next age of digital publishing." — SE

wired.com/app

IMAGE © CONDE NAST

Condé Nast and Wired magazine have pushed the possibilities of iPad-optimised content further than most publishers. Specialist content includes individually-designed pages to suit portrait or landscape orientations and material developed with a touch screen device in mind, such as animated 360-degree images. Content is organised in a structure which works with the format rather than as traditional magazine-like pages. Developed in collaboration with Adobe, the original US version offered a first glimpse of the possibilities of online publishing, with Wired UK following in December 2010. It is still too early to tell whether the app will eventually replace the printed magazine but the content is significantly different enough to be an experience in itself. Apps like this have certainly demonstrated that an online paywall version of a print format is a workable proposition.

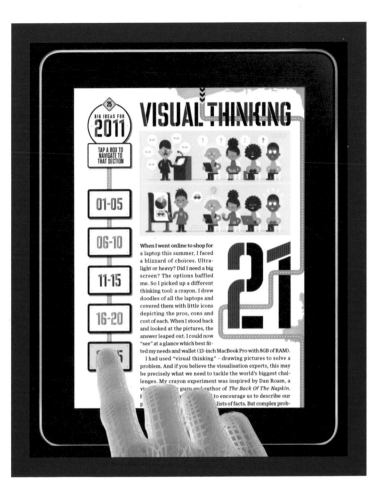

25
BIG IDEAS FOR
2011

TAP A BOX TO
NAVIGATE TO
THAT SECTION

01-05

06-10

11-15

16-20

VISUAL THINKING

21

When I went online to shop for a laptop this summer, I faced a blizzard of choices. Ultra-light or heavy? Did I need a big screen? The options baffled me. So I picked up a different thinking tool: a crayon. I drew doodles of all the laptops and covered them with little icons depicting the pros, cons and cost of each. When I stood back and looked at the pictures, the answer leaped out. I could now "see" at a glance which best fitted my needs and wallet (13-inch MacBook Pro with 8GB of RAM).

I had used "visual thinking" – drawing pictures to solve a problem. And if you believe the visualisation experts, this may be precisely what we need to tackle the world's biggest challenges. My crayon experiment was inspired by Dan Roam, a visualising guru and author of *The Back Of The Napkin*. For centuries we've been told to encourage us to describe our problems as lists of facts. But complex prob-

PRODUCT

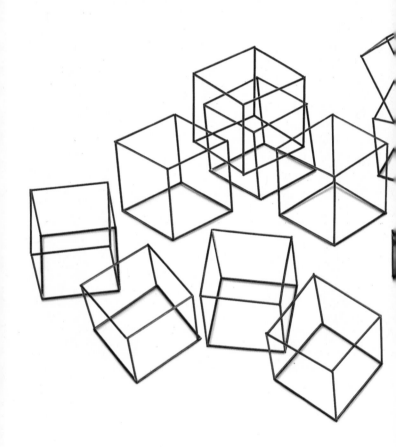

ACT FIRE EXTINGUISHER

Designed by SIGRUN VIK

☆ Nominated by ANNA THORUD HAMMER: "The Act fire extinguisher integrates a number of new solutions, within the modernisation of a safety product that concerns us all. Using existing technology in innovative ways alongside brand new technologies, the extinguisher reacts with light and sound when the fire alarm is activated and warns the user by SMS when the contents need replacing. The ability to use the product with one hand represents a major advance and the aesthetics are very appealing compared to existing devices." — ATH

sigrunvikdesign.com

IMAGE © PEDER TORGET

The concept of fire safety and fire extinguishers can feel intimidating to many. People don't know where extinguishers are positioned, how to use them or how to take care of them. These challenges were the basis for the Act project, a new concept for an intelligent fire extinguisher. Act is designed to fit within the modern home and lifestyle, striking a balance between intuitive functions and discreet appearance. Most fire extinguishers are deliberately designed to be visually intrusive for easy identification in an emergency. Act avoids this by connecting to a wireless fire alarm system and alerting users with sound and light emitted from the extinguisher when the alarm is triggered. Instead of confusing meters and gauges, Act sends the user SMS text messages when a service is needed.

PRODUCT: USA

AMPLIFY CHANDELIER

Designed by YVES BEHAR // FUSEPROJECT
for SWAROVSKI

☆ Nominated by MICHELLE OGUNDEHIN: "Amplify articulates Yves Béhar's goal of uniting technology, emotion, accessibility and sustainability. Amplify combines one crystal and one low-energy LED light within a simple, frameless, faceted paper shade. 'It is a pursuit in my work to try to achieve the maximum effect with the minimum amount of materials and energy,' explains Béhar. 'The challenge was how to achieve the magical effect of many crystals on a chandelier: could we amplify a single crystal to create an entire chandelier?' The answer is yes. Six different shapes, each carefully crafted to maximise refractions on the inner surfaces of the shade, mean each light becomes a large glowing paper crystal. Presented in a cost-effective, flat-pack package, Amplify is, as Béhar puts it, 'truly the simplest, most attainable crystal chandelier'." — MO

fuseproject.com/products-46
swarovskicrystalpalace.com

IMAGE © FUSEPROJECT

Amplify is a crystal lighting collaboration with Swarovski, which launched at the 2010 Salone del Mobile. Traditional chandeliers are made of numerous lights and crystals. Yves Béhar and fuseproject changed this equation to one crystal, one LED light and one faceted paper shade. The result is multiple beautiful reflections and the rainbow colour burst associated with chandeliers, achieved through the amplification of just one crystal. Using low-energy LEDs and FSC-certified paper shades, and produced using green energy, the lighting series is as sustainable as it is beautiful.

APPLE iPAD

Designed by APPLE

☆ Nominated by PATICK BURGOYNE // SEBASTIAN CONRAN // JEREMY LESLIE // LYNDA RELPH-KNIGHT // DAVID ROWAN: "It hardly seems possible that a product on the UK market for barely eight months has had such an impact on the digital fraternity as well as Apple's bottom line. Timing is everything. Maybe a year earlier and the battery life and screen resolution would not have been as good. A year later and a competitor would have taken root. Less than a decade ago iBooks were translucent coloured plastic-organic forms. Now the iPad is a tactile anodised aluminium aerofoil. In five years time who knows what it will be." — SC

"Already, the iPad is changing the way we look at things online, and it will have a particularly significant impact on the publishing industry. Handheld devices aren't new — and nor are the apps hitting the iPad as they did with the iPhone — but this is a genuinely consumer-facing technology product. It opens up so many new ways of doing things creatively, from content and visuals to ads, and liberates users to access more stuff of high quality when, and more or less where, they choose. You can browse online at last." — LR-K

apple.com/ipad

IMAGE © APPLE

The iPad is the first genuinely usable and consumer-facing tablet computer. While previous devices relied on clunky interfaces operated with a stylus, the iPad offers the Multi-Touch user interface and the operating system used by the iPhone. However, for a product to be a success it must also be useful. The iPad has succeeded, not because it performs tasks that can't be carried out on other devices, but because it performs them in a way that is more intuitive, enjoyable and engaging. The appearance and industrial design takes cues from a number of other Apple products, using brushed aluminium, black surrounds and bevelled corners. The result is an object that is covetous, light enough to be truly portable and, most important of all, genuinely useful.

BLUEWARE COLLECTION

Designed by STUDIO GLITHERO
Developed with VAUXHALL COLLECTIVE

☆ Nominated by HENRIETTA THOMPSON: "The work of Studio Glithero is exceptional in its celebration of the process behind its products — often installations and videos showing the making of their designs are as important as the products themselves. Blueware is no exception: reviving and adapting the blueprinting process, a dying art from the Victorian period of great discoveries when British explorers travelled the world in search of exotic new species. In 1840 chemist and botanist John Herschel invented blueprinting, marking the advent of photography and offering his fellow pioneers an invaluable tool to record and document their discoveries. Inspired by this, the intrepid Studio Glithero travelled to the UK's centre for ceramic heritage, Stoke-on-Trent, and worked with master ceramicists to create an innovative process bringing together an artisan approach to ceramics with a rare use of photography." — HT

studioglithero.com

IMAGE © PETR KREJCI

Studio Glithero has invented a process that captures direct impressions of botanical specimens on ceramics using light and photosensitive chemicals. It is similar to the early photographic printing technique known as blueprinting. Using age-old preserving techniques, humble weeds from inner-London pavements are pressed, dried and then delicately composed on the surface of a vase or tile. Working with light sensitive chemicals, the objects are exposed for several hours under ultraviolet light, which develops a photogram of the pattern in intense Prussian blue. What remains is a crisp white silhouette of the specimen, creating an intricate impression of the subject from root to tip.

153

CONTEMPLATING MONOLITHIC DESIGN

Created by SONY DESIGN // BARBEROSGERBY
Exhibition design by UNIVERSAL DESIGN STUDIO

☆ Nominated by by ZOE RYAN: "London-based designers Edward Barber and Jay Osgerby perceive the practice of design as a creative and cultural endeavour in which experiments bring about innovation. For the Sony exhibition in Milan, BarberOsgerby created an installation based on research into new archetypes of objects for the home, and incorporated the latest technology in sound and light. Housed within a tactile acoustic chamber, the sculptural objects explore how materials, including wood, plastic and glass, generate a range of sound and light conditions and, through their placement, different spatial conditions within the environment. Providing insights into the relationship with audio and video systems in our daily lives, the installation made apparent the experiential aspects of design and its powerful engagement with senses beyond sight and touch alone." — ZR

barberosgerby.com

IMAGE © SONY

Contemplating Monolithic Design at the 2010 Salone del Mobile presented a future vision of electronics design, merged with furniture and home architecture. Sony designers worked with BarberOsgerby to explore the integration of products within contemporary lifestyles, expressed through conceptual archetypes. The installation was an all-encompassing, fully immersive experience constructed in a space designed to eliminate superficial sounds and views. Acoustic foam wedges of varying heights formed this anechoic landscape, while the diverse archetypes on display included lighting, furniture and architecture, illustrating the potential for the pieces to blend seamlessly into any setting. Sony and BarberOsgerby's collaborative creative thinking was demonstrated throughout, offering visitors the chance to experience how technology and design could shape the living room of the future.

155

PRODUCT: DENMARK

DIAMANT COFFIN SERIES

Designed by JACOB JENSEN DESIGN
Manufactured by TOMMERUP KISTER

☆ Nominated by HENRIETTA THOMPSON: "For those after a more sophisticated send-off there has traditionally been little choice when it comes to coffins. Still an area surrounded by some taboo, death is not something designers have dwelled on for long. Jacob Jensen Studio wanted to redress this, thinking outside the box with the Diamant series of coffins and urns. Created with the more contemporary funeral in mind, the collection is the result of a two year collaboration with coffin manufacturer Tommerup Kister and brings a new elegance of form and functionality to the product category. Sculptural inspiration for the multifaceted design came from the diamond. The highest point in the coffin follows the heart line, where its surface is such that a single flower can be placed on it." — HT

jacobjensen.com
tommerup-kister.dk

IMAGE © TOMMERUP KISTER

The Diamant series is a line of universal, timeless coffins and urns where form and emotion unite to provide a dignified farewell. Presenting a marked break with the past, the series draws on Tommerup Kister's 100 years of funeral directing and Jacob Jensen Design's 50 years of design tradition. Inspiration comes from the structure and facets of a diamond, which Jensen considers to be a poetic symbol of the perpetual, pure and exalted. From concept to production the process lasted more than two years and involved 75 prototypes. The coffins are made by local Danish craftsmen and are assembled by hand from Nordic birch ply, a more sustainable alternative to traditional hardwoods. They are available in black or white lacquer finish, with a hand finished interior upholstered in organic cotton.

DYSON
AIR MULTIPLIER FAN

Designed by JAMES DYSON

☆ Nominated by SEBASTIAN CONRAN: "Questioning something that is taken for granted often drives invention and innovation. Why do vacuum cleaners need bags? Why do hand dryers take so long? Why do fans need to be so clumsy? And how do you make the familiar more desirable? Traditionally fan technology hasn't changed much since Edwardian times, and then only to make the product easier and cheaper to manufacture, rather than better for the consumer. Using the technology of the carburettor, the aerofoil and sophisticated engineering harnessed by elegant industrial design is what makes this product different and appealing. It is something to want as well as need. It does a demonstrably better job, whilst not having to apologise for its appearance, which is refreshingly minimal. It is to fans what Richard Sapper's Tizio lamp was to task lighting." — SC

dyson.co.uk/fans

IMAGE © DYSON

The blades on a conventional fan chop the air as they spin, causing uneven airflow and constant buffeting. This always disappointed James Dyson, who set about developing a fan that didn't rely on blades. His Air Multiplier technology amplifies the surrounding air, giving an uninterrupted stream of smooth air. Drawn in by an energy-efficient brushless motor, air is accelerated through the circular loop of the fan and passes over an airfoil-shaped ramp that channels and directs its flow. Air behind and around the fan is then pulled into the airflow and amplified. As a result of hundreds of simulations run by Dyson's fluid dynamics engineers, the Dyson Air Multiplier Fan amplifies incoming air 15 times, expelling 405 litres of smooth and uninterrupted air every second – all without the need for blades.

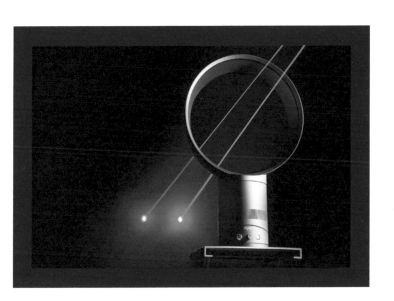

159

FREECOM CLS MOBILE DRIVE

Designed by SYLVAIN WILLENZ
Manufactured by FREECOM

☆ Nominated by ARIC CHEN: "Organising and managing data is one of the biggest challenges of our time. The April 2010 announcement that the US Library of Congress would store the entire Twitter archive only prompted the question of how anyone could possibly make sense of it all. On an individual level, the data problem can seem equally overwhelming, which is why the Freecom CLS external hard drive by Sylvain Willenz is so compelling. Essentially, it allows you to create a library in the old-fashioned, physical mould. Data is stored, organised — and labelled — on any number of cartridge-like drives, any three of which can be connected to a single dock at one time. It is totally intuitive." — AC

freecom.com
sylvainwillenz.com

IMAGE © JULIEN RENAULT

The CLS Mobile Drive is an external mobile hard drive with a labelling system that enables users to organise data and identify hard drive contents at a glance. Witnessing the growing number of hard drives owned by individuals to store music, films and back-ups — and taking inspiration from old cassette tapes and floppy drives — Sylvain Willenz imagined a drive that could be catalogued in a simple and personal way. The result is a label kept behind a removable window set in the side of the drive. The CLS comes in a stackable see-through case with spare coloured labels and a small USB cable. Alongside, Willenz has also designed a dock, allowing for three drives and one extra peripheral device to be connected to the computer simultaneously.

FLYING FUTURE

Designed by INGO MAURER

☆ Nominated by FRANCESCA PICCHI: "Flying Future is not only the first application of OLED technology in a domestic object, its formal solution envisions the future of light as an object in itself: a luminous lighting surface floating freely in the air. In the organic version of LEDs the light is emitted not from a point, as in standard LEDs, but from a surface. The light source doesn't blind and is cold enough to touch, so you can directly manipulate it. Although still in an experimental phase, Ingo Maurer and his team have set a formal reference for future OLED development." — FP

ingo-maurer.com

IMAGE © INGO MAURER // TOM VACK

Flying Future is the realisation of a long-cherished dream that began with experimental organic LED (OLED) lighting designs in 2006 and 2008. Flying Future uses 90 Novaled OLED modules set into a large transparent plastic sheet in a gridded pattern. The modules are created from glass substrates which render them transparent when switched off, creating the effect of a delicate cloth floating in the air and moving in the wind. Ingo Maurer has used LEDs since their introduction in the early 1980s and believes OLED technology is an exciting gift for lighting design, with an impact as major as LED or halogen lamps. Maurer's interest lies not only in technological progress but also in how new technologies bring about change in the formal aspects of products, leading to new forms.

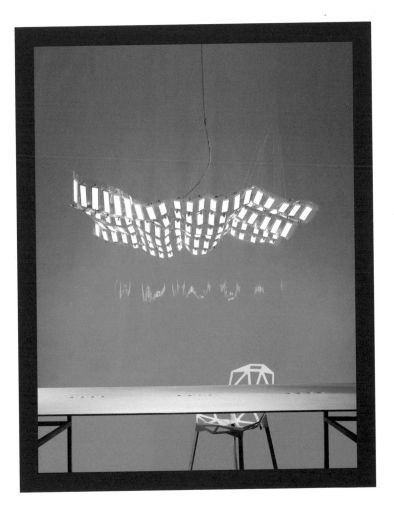

IN-BETWEENING CLOCK

Designed by HYE-YEON PARK

☆ Nominated by GARETH WILLIAMS: "Hye-Yeon Park's compelling In-betweening Clock reveals the interstices between recorded moments of time by morphing each digit into the next. Now we see time ebbing and flowing. In all other respects the clock works like a regular 24 hour digital clock, with hour, minute and second displays. Before joining the Royal College of Art, Hye-Yeon Park studied industrial design at Hongik University, Korea." — GW

hyeonpark.com

IMAGE © HYE-YEON PARK

The In-betweening Clock visualises time as a series of numbers melting into one another. Time, as we know, is a human construct, and the way in which we tell the time is an artificial code. While the sweeping arms of an analogue clock may suggest the flow of time, this is not the case with digital displays, which switch crisply from digit to digit, and moment to moment. Taking its name from an animation technique that creates the necessary 'in-between' frames when given a starting and end image, Hye-Yeon Park's clock generates frames between the fixed moments of time displayed by digital clocks. The concept illustrates the continuous flow evident in analogue devices, such as sundials or egg-timers, and also explores the graphic form of numbers.

INTIMATERIDER

Designed by ALAN THOLKES

☆ Nominated by DANIEL CHARNY: "If you agree that design should mediate between who we are and the world around us, and that good design actually betters people's lives, then IntimateRider qualifies as a wonderful piece of design. Intelligent mechanical thinking and an unassuming ubiquitous support structure allow for a gliding motion that enables sexual positioning and movement for disabled men and women. Users' lives have obviously been the centre of attention for the design team. Thoughtfully lightweight, the product fits into a carry case and is also supported by an online blog (www.intimaterider. com/home/blog) discussing the psychological and social aspects of long term or temporary disability and sexual life. A useful, innovative, thoughtful and inclusive product." — DC

intimaterider.com

IMAGE © INTIMATERIDER

IntimateRider is the only product on the market designed to enhance sexual mobility for those with limited or no lower body muscle control. Originally designed by a C6-7 quadriplegic for his own personal use, the designer wanted to provide a natural fluid motion that would help people with an assortment of physical challenges in their intimate relationships. No motors or springs are used; just a gentle movement of the head or upper body is enough to set the small swing chair in motion. The device is light and easy to move, folds for compact storage and features non-skid glides and stable back support.

LEVERAGED FREEDOM CHAIR

Designed by MIT MOBILITY LABORATORY
Developed in collaboration with ASSOCIATION FOR THE
PHYSICALLY DISABLED IN KENYA // BMVSS JAIPUR //
CONTINUUM // INDIAN INSTITUTE OF TECHNOLOGY
DELHI // TRANSITIONS FOUNDATION OF GUATEMALA //
WHIRLWIND WHEELCHAIR INTERNATIONAL

☆ Nominated by DANIEL CHARNY: "Design based
on a deep understanding of their many users' needs,
environment and economic means makes the LFC a
spectacular product. It is also impressive for tackling
such a strong existing design. Learning from both
mountain bikes and office chairs has produced a clear
ingenious break from the wheelchair norm. Constructed
from widely available, cheap bicycle parts, the
LFC features two large levers attached to a bicycle
drivetrain that helps the chair power through mud and
over rocky paths. The design has been developed and
tested with full user consultation in East Africa and
has attracted interest from Uganda, Guatemala and
Jaipur. The LFC isn't just about independent access
and social mobility, it is also accessible." — DC

mlab.mit.edu/lfc

IMAGE © MIT MOBILITY LAB

The Leveraged Freedom Chair
(LFC) is a mobility aid designed
specifically for people with
disabilities in developing
countries. For most of this
population, the only connections
to education, employment,
and community are via long
distances on dirt roads and
walking paths — terrains too
harsh for existing mobility
products. The LFC has a variable
mechanical advantage lever
drivetrain that enables its user
to travel 10-20 per cent faster
on tarmac than a conventional
wheelchair, and off-road like
few other mobility aids. The
user changes gear by moving
their hand position on the
levers. Grasping high increases
leverage, grasping low makes
the chair go faster. Removing
the levers and stowing them
within the frame transforms
the LFC into a conventional
wheelchair for indoor use. All
moving parts are made from
bicycle components found in any
developing country, making the
LFC cheap and easy to build and
repair anywhere in the world.

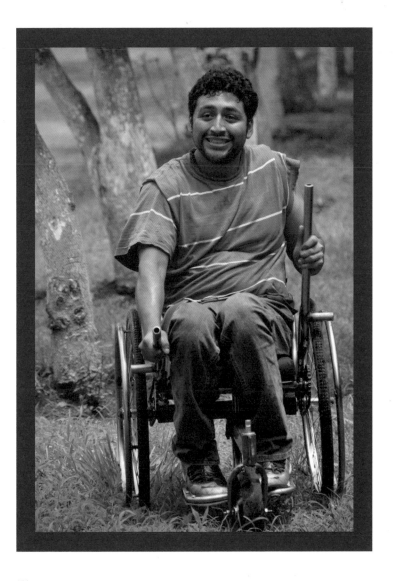

ONE ARM DRIVE SYSTEM

Designed and developed by JON OWEN // MARK OWEN
Manufactured by NOMAD WHEELCHAIRS LTD

☆ Nominated by DAVID ROWAN: "The One Arm Drive by Nomad is a sleek, compact wheelchair that, as the name suggests, can be moved using one hand. It shows that design for disabled people needn't be clunky and ugly. It's got a sense of 'cool' and is easy to manoeuvre. It's lightweight yet strong — made from aircraft-grade aluminium — and designed to be practical, with quick-release wheels. You can see that Nomad co-founder Mark Owen, who uses a wheelchair after an accident, really understands what the user needs." — DR

---

nomadwheelchairs.com/one-arm-drive

IMAGE © PHIL BOORMAN PHOTOGRAPHY

Nomad founders, wheelchair user Mark Owen and his brother Jon, believe function has led form in the mobility industry for too long. Setting out to challenge this tradition, their latest product drives both wheels of a wheelchair from a single side, ideal for users with limited mobility in one hand or arm. Lightweight and reliable engineering keeps weight low and performance levels up, while Nomad's commitment to style ensures the One Arm Drive looks great. The lightweight components are mostly aluminium, with some parts heat treated to prepare them for years of demanding use. Various forms of machining, from laserjet cutting to milling and reaming, are used in the production. And a degree of customisation allows for parts to be anodised in various colours.

PAVEGEN

Designed by LAURENCE KEMBALL-COOK //
PHILIP TUCKER

☆ Nominated by SEBASTIAN CONRAN: "Do you ever wonder how much energy you lose into the pavement when you walk down the street? Every time someone steps on these paving slabs, the surface depresses slightly. This tiny movement can generate up to seven watts of electrical power, or 32.4 kilowatts an hour in a busy area. At night about five per cent of the generated power is used to illuminate a bright LED light and the rest can be stored in a self-contained battery. Designed to replace conventional paving with minimum disruption, this technology could also be applied to stairs, speed bumps or any area where road traffic is likely to be slowing down. The off grid approach means paved areas can be self-lighting, storing power during the day and only lighting up at night." — SC

pavegensystems.com

IMAGE © SCIENCE MUSEUM, LONDON

Pavegen paving slabs harness the energy generated from footsteps to power street lighting, signage and information displays. The top rubber panel flexes around 5mm with each impact, sparking internal components to convert this kinetic movement into electrical energy. Five per cent of the produced power is used to make the slab light up. The remaining 95 per cent can run low-power applications, such as streetlights, pedestrian lights, shop fronts, wayfinding solutions, interactive and educational displays. The rubber surface made from recycled car tyres provides a durable, low maintenance alternative to concrete paving. And a zero-carbon concrete or stainless steel outer structure prevents corrosion from gritting and rainfall.

PLAYING WITH LEGO®
BRICKS AND PAPER

Designed by MUJI // LEGO

☆ Nominated by SAM HECHT: "I love LEGO – it allows a child to feel the thread of construction, destruction and reconstruction over and over again, with no end point. But it's become quite a different toy nowadays because of the enormous marketing energy put into themed products like Star Wars, where there is a very clear end point. So, to see LEGO collaborate with Muji is very interesting, because Muji is about the unthemed experience. With the combination of a hole punch that shares the same pitch as a LEGO piece, it returns LEGO to a commodity that can be shaped purely by imagination, free from any prescribed theme." — SH

muji.com/lego

IMAGE © THE LEGO GROUP // MUJI

LEGO Bricks and Paper is a collaboration between Japanese retailer Muji and Danish manufacturer LEGO. The two organisations explored how various combinations of artistic activities stimulated new forms of creative play, with the aim of developing a LEGO brick-based product to help parents engage in creative craft play with their children. As a result, the LEGO system paper puncher enables children and parents to draw, colour in, cut out and put together paper or card creations using LEGO bricks. The open-ended possibilities and the need for imaginative responses emphasise the idea that LEGO bricks are more than a construction toy. Initially a small-scale project launched in selected Japanese Muji stores, its immediate success led to further testing and development before a later version was produced for distribution elsewhere in the world.

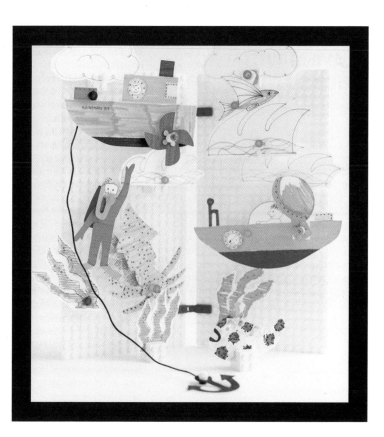

175

PLUMEN 001

Concept and design direction by HULGER
Designed by SAMUEL WILKINSON

☆ Nominated by SAM HECHT // SHANE WALTER: "A masterclass in using imaginative design to transform something of bland utility into a thing of coveted beauty, which then becomes more usable and more enjoyable. Plumen makes the bare bulb chic, mixing the ecological with a design style full of wit, energy and personality to emanate a low-energy glow in both the room and your conscience. What is terrific about Hulger is that it challenges accepted norms. Light bulbs are a commodity item sold in high volume with no interest from manufacturers to change them. As founder Nic Roope puts it, 'it's strange that the bulb, an object so synonymous with ideas, is almost entirely absent of imagination'. Not any more." — SW

hulger.com
plumen.com
samwilkinson.co.uk

IMAGE © HULGER

Plumen is poles apart from low-energy light bulbs as we know them. Rather than hiding the unappealing compact fluorescent light behind boring utility, Plumen 001 is designed as an object the owner would want to show off. The glass tubes take an irregular yet harmonious form, the two organic shapes mirror one another to create symmetry, and the silhouette changes from every perspective. The name derives from a bird's decorative 'plume' feathers, designed to attract attention, and the word for a unit of light, 'lumen'. The bulb uses 80 per cent less energy and lasts eight times longer than traditional incandescent bulbs and works just like any low-energy bulb. Sold as a design object rather than a commodity, premium materials and processes are used, delivering the best possible quality of light.

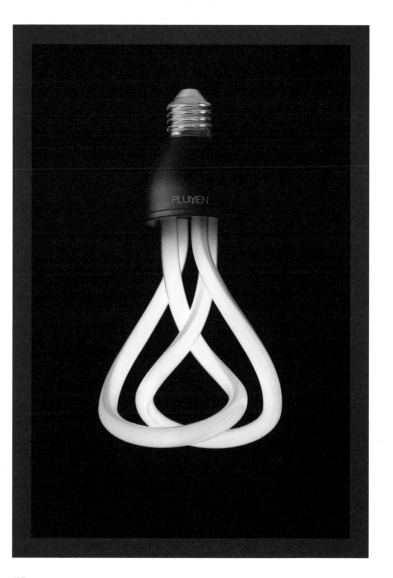

PRAMPACK

Designed by KADABRA PRODUKTDESIGN
Invented by ANNE MORKEMO
Manufactured by STOKKE

☆ Nominated by ANNA THORUD HAMMER: "PramPack offers the first universal and functional solution to a common problem. The product fits most pushchairs and takes up very little space when not in use. Its sporty, robust design provides good protection against rough handling and the signal colours make the key functions visible to ground crew as well as creating a strong identity. A highly innovative product within this sector, PramPack has grabbed the attention of the industry and generated considerable interest." — ATH

kadabra.com
prampack.com

IMAGE © STOKKE AS

PramPack is a wheeled bag designed for the protection of prams during transportation. It fits almost all types of prams, and can be rolled up when not in use. Inspired by the continuous damage her seven month old son's pram sustained during air transportation on a round-the-world trip, inventor Anne Morkemo decided to research the issue. Both airline companies and other travelling parents confirmed no good solution existed. Morkemo also discovered that tens of thousands of prams were destroyed each year during air transportation. In cooperation with Scandinavian airline companies, parents and industrial designers, she set out to create a product that would make travelling with small children and a pram easier. Six prototypes later, PramPack has been tested and approved by several airlines.

QUARZ SERIES

Designed by MAX LAMB
Manufactured by LOBMEYR

☆ Nominated by THOMAS GEISLER: "These Lobmeyr tumblers derive from an experimental project exploring the value created by craftsmanship in a range of production methods applied to glass. Working from an excel spreadsheet, Max Lamb poetically transforms business data into glass objects. The Quarz series is the most promising output of this process, which realises measures of labour, material and skills within a marketable, handcrafted and high quality commercial object." — TG

lobmeyr.at
maxlamb.org

IMAGE © QUARZ

Max Lamb's Quarz is a series of crystal tumblers representing perfect mathematical prisms. The shapes mirror the hexagonal prisms formed when quartz — the main raw material for glass production — grows in an uninhibited space. Quarz also references the German spelling of the mineral, reflecting manufacturer Lobmeyr's Austrian roots. Each Quarz tumbler is mouth blown into the same cylindrical wooden mould then cut at three assorted heights, providing variation within a manufactured production process. The hand-cut and polished hexagonal facets allow the glasses to be arranged in a Giant's Causeway-type landscape, creating a glass model of the geological formation on the Northern Irish coast renowned for its hexagonal basalt columns.

SEE BETTER TO LEARN BETTER

Designed by YVES BEHAR // FUSEPROJECT
in partnership with AUGEN OPTICS

☆ Nominated by MICHELLE OGUNDEHIN: "Fuseproject's Yves Béhar says his role as a designer is 'about ideas and how to realise those ideas in the most beautiful and communicative way'. Easy to say, harder to do, but beautifully articulated with See Better to Learn Better, the free eyeglasses programme for children. It not only provided sight to those that really needed it, by offering free eye exams alongside the glasses, it overcame an endemic local stigma to the wearing of spectacles. Béhar created a product that children could personalise, choosing the style and colour of their specs themselves, which made them desirable and fun as well as functional. To me this was pure design, design conceived to solve a problem and be aesthetically-pleasing at the same time." — MO

augenoptics.com
fuseproject.com

IMAGE © FUSEPROJECT

See Better to Learn Better is a free children's eyeglasses programme developed in partnership with the Mexican government and Augen Optics. The collaboration has led to a collection of customisable and stylish corrective eyewear specifically designed for 6-18 year old students. The aim is to provide spectacles for children whose families are unable to afford the cost of eye care. Yves Béhar and fuseproject concentrated on designing products suited to the children's specific needs, life and environment, creating frames that were both durable and ergonomic. By customising elements such as shape and colour, wearing the glasses becomes a fun and personal experience.

UNIVERSAL GOWN

Designed by BEN DE LISI

☆ Nominated by DAVID KESTER: "Why must hospital gowns open at the back? It's an issue that doesn't just leave you feeling a little exposed and a bit cold. Experiencing worry or discomfort in hospital can affect your ability to get better. That, in turn, affects hospital staff and NHS costs. It's a problem that has eluded designers until this year, when the Department of Health commissioned the Design for Patient Dignity initiative. The project gave fashion designer Ben de Lisi the opportunity to work with NHS professionals and patients to come up with a new hospital gown that's comfy, competitively priced and dignified. We will all have personal experience of being in hospital and when it's my turn I know I'll be grateful that designers have had the opportunity to deliver this new gown." — DK

bendelisi.com

IMAGE © DESIGN COUNCIL

Unlike existing hospital garments, Ben de Lisi's overhaul of the standard NHS gown covers both the front and back of the patient. The Universal Gown opens and closes down both sides and across one shoulder, fastening with polymer press-studs that provide access for IV drips and other equipment without exposing the patient's skin. Completely reversible, nursing staff can place the press-stud openings on the side nearest to any bedside equipment, while the polycotton fabric with soft jersey at the neck and shoulders is designed for comfort and ease of movement. Additional side panels can also be fitted to accommodate large patients, making this single gown flexible enough to replace a range of traditional hospital attire. The Universal Gown is already in demand from NHS Trusts and international healthcare organisations.

WALL PIERCING

Designed by RON GILAD
Manufactured by FLOS

☆ Nominated by PAOLA ANTONELLI // ZOE RYAN:
"Aptly named, Ron Gilad's Wall Piercing appears to penetrate the wall from which it hangs, tacked on simply like a piercing. However, these fixtures are actually connected to plaster panels integrated into the wall, so that the wall itself becomes a pure surface on which light and shadows are cast from the circular lamps. The innovative designs use LED technology and are manufactured by Flos. They can be mounted in multiple ways and offer colour variation and dimming to create different lighting atmospheres. Gilad has long been interested in the expressive qualities of objects and here challenges preconceptions about how light affects our immediate surroundings." — ZR

rongilad.com
soft-architecture.com

IMAGE © MICHAEL LOOS

Wall Piercing is part of Italian lighting manufacturer Flos' Soft Architecture range of innovative lighting products. Designed by Israeli-born, New York-based artist Ron Gilad, the circular lamp uses composite materials to seamlessly blend its fixtures into its surroundings and become part of the physical structure of a building. Each individual piercing is an austere hoop of LEDs lodged shallowly into a wall, which diffuses its own shadow to give the appearance of being shrouded in a light tulle fog. By linking multiple units, a pattern of light can be woven across a surface, with each piercing serving as a single 'pixel' in a larger image. An entire 'pierced' wall or ceiling can alter the appearance and mood of its environment with each shift in the colour and intensity of light.

YII

Conceived by NATIONAL TAIWAN CRAFT RESEARCH INSTITUTE (NTCRI) // TAIWAN DESIGN CENTER (TDC)
Creative direction by GIJS BAKKER

☆ Nominated by FRANCESCA PICCHI: "Yii aims to give new and international life to the image of eastern traditional objects through a combination of skilful handmade craftsmanship and mass-production processes. In the Panlong Vase (designed by Chen-hsu Liu with the collaboration of craft artist Shi-ren Lu) classical dragons and tigers made using traditional Koji pottery and ceramic techniques are combined with the computer-designed geometric shape of the vase body. Pieces from the IKEA plus series (conceived by designer Pili Wu) unite the neutrality of industrial everyday objects with the visionary freedom of craft." — FP

yiidesign.com

IMAGE © WILLIAM CHEN

In Taiwanese philosophy Yii, meaning change and transformation, is believed to be the underlying law of nature. Taking this as inspiration, Yii is an ambitious design project conceived by the National Taiwan Craft Research Institute and the Taiwan Design Center. It aims to create strong and sustainable links between local Taiwanese craft traditions and contemporary design practice in Taiwan. The first Yii collection draws on the intuitive wisdom of ancient culture, where a focus is placed on skilful craftsmanship and manufacturing processes deeply rooted in a harmonious relation between man and nature. The pieces include 'embroidered lace' porcelain bowls, a silkworm-cocooned stool and Starbucks coffee cups made from basketwork, ceramics and blown glass.

TRANSPORT

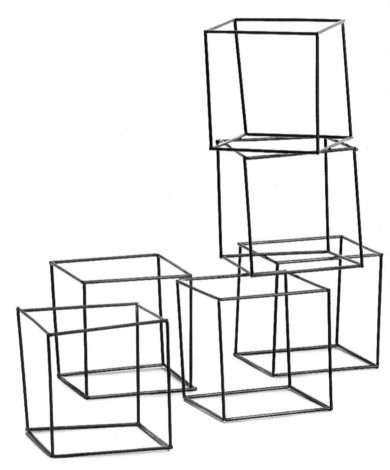

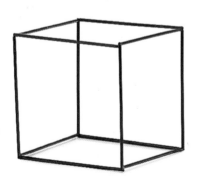

BARCLAYS CYCLE HIRE

TRANSPORT FOR LONDON // SERCO

☆ Nominated by SEBASTIAN CONRAN // WAYNE HEMINGWAY MBE // WILL HUDSON: "I use this scheme two or three times a week. It's affordable, simple to use and well-managed. The bikes are solid, the strap and basket hold my briefcase safely and the docking system ensures minimal theft. Most importantly it helps to add a critical mass of cyclists to a city which needs to encourage car drivers (and especially taxi drivers) to be more tolerant of the cycling 'massive'. A triumph and a welcome addition to this great city." — WH MBE

tfl.gov.uk/roadusers/cycling/14808.aspx

IMAGE © TRANSPORT FOR LONDON

Launched in summer 2010, the Barclays Cycle Hire scheme has quickly become a popular and familiar feature across London. The user-friendly and robust cycles are the scheme's most obvious customer-facing element. Features include dynamo-powered lights which remain on at traffic lights, adjustable saddles, luggage racks which avoid gathering litter and chain guards.

The success of the scheme, however, is not down to the cycle alone. The other design elements combine to form an integrated and coherent whole. Docking stations are distinctive enough to be recognisable, yet unobtrusive enough to blend in with an urban landscape encompassing city skyscrapers and Royal Parks. Terminals incorporate Legible London mapping, benefitting both cyclists and pedestrians. And the carefully designed pricing structure and animated marketing characters have been instrumental in the scheme's rapid take-up.

DEZIR

Designed by LAURENS VAN DEN ACKER for RENAULT

☆ Nominated by DALE HARROW: "Car design is a complex mix of rational and emotional aspects, combined to create a product that exerts an emotional pull on the consumer. The shape of the DeZir electric vehicle concept is reminiscent of sports cars (it is even painted red in homage to another famous brand) and there is little to suggest that it is powered by anything other than a conventional engine. The success of the design is in the quality and completeness of the solution, including the interior. The car has many features that would be expected on a typical concept car, such as asymmetric scissor doors, slimline LED headlights and a paint-splattered interior. Renault's designers have produced a truly breathtaking piece of automotive sculpture, which connects the past with the future." — DH

renault.com

IMAGE © RENAULT

Under the leadership of Laurens van den Acker, Renault's design department have produced a concept car which bucks the perceived view of electric cars. Deliberately styled with expressive passion and emotion it has a flamboyant yet composed appearance. A pair of reverse-hinged butterfly doors demonstrate the showy side, while the smooth sculptural fluidity of the Kevlar body panels represents Renault's new vision of 'simple, sensuous and warm'. Though its performance won't rival the combustion-driven supercars of old, DeZir can still reach 100km/h in under five seconds, with a range of 160km from a single charge. The system generates kinetic energy from deceleration, storing it in the battery for later use. Three charging methods allow the driver to use a conventional household plug, a fast-charge station, or quickly and easily swap an entire battery.

EN-V

Designed by GENERAL MOTORS

☆ Nominated by DALE HARROW: "EN-V provides a solution to future urban mobility and moves vehicle design from product to service. The system-based design uses a convergence of communication and electronic technology to enable self-driving vehicles to navigate and provide personal mobility in increasingly population-dense city environments. The EN-V's atypical, short, upright proportion offers a high seating position with good access to the interior and improved visibility. The autonomous operating capability offers the promise of reduced traffic congestion, by allowing EN-Vs to automatically select the fastest route based on real-time traffic information. Safety is improved for all road users due to advances in sensing technology and communication between EN-Vs that responds to other road users and pedestrians." — DH

gm.com

IMAGE © GM CORPORATION

The EN-V or Electric-Networked Vehicle is a concept designed to meet the demands of an increasing urban population. The three models, Jiao (Pride), Miao (Magic) and Xiao (Laugh), follow on from prototypes developed in collaboration with Segway. Two passengers and light luggage fit in a vehicle about a third the size of a traditional car, which can turn by rotating on a central point. Drive-by-wire technology with interfaces similar to video games replaces the traditional mechanical control systems, while networked connectivity allows automated and autonomous driving, parking and retrieval. The concept employs social networking principles to enable communication between drivers, occupants and others on the go. GM Motors hopes this combination of sensing technology, wireless communication and GPS-based navigation will lead the way to future advanced vehicle safety systems.

FIAT 500 TWINAIR

Designed by FIAT

☆ Nominated by DALE HARROW: "The original Fiat 500, designed by Dante Giacosa in 1957, was a masterpiece of industrial design born out of a post-war landscape where materials and money were scarce. In today's era of rising economic consciousness the new Fiat 500 TwinAir goes back to its origins, employing radical solutions to produce a car with a bespoke twin cylinder engine, improvements of up to 30 per cent in fuel consumption and class leading CO_2 output. This represents a genuine alternative to electric cars and the future direction for internal combustion engine development. The TwinAir is a thoroughly modern small car with high standards of manufacture, safety, equipment and usability, all wrapped in a retro cool package and 'fall-in-love' detailing inside and out. The 500 is a cult car, which shows that amazing advances are possible in the practical efficiency of small cars." — DH

twinair.fiat500.com

IMAGE © FIAT

At a time when the remodelling of past small cars proved popular around the world, the retro styling of the Fiat 500 a few years ago earned Roberto Giolito and the Fiat design team a host of awards. The latest model now has an engine to match its looks: the innovative two-cylinder TwinAir, the greenest and most efficient petrol engine built to date. A two-cylinder engine is unconventional, but has heritage, since the original 500 was also powered by twin cylinders. This radical new engine offers improvements of up to 30 per cent in fuel consumption and CO_2 output, and is just the start of Fiat's two-cylinder plans. A petrol-electric hybrid version of the TwinAir is due to enter production in the near future.

RIVERSIMPLE

Designed by RIVERSIMPLE

☆ Nominated by MARK ADAMS: "The car industry is on the cusp of a major transformation, and one which must go way beyond replacing the internal combustion engine. What I love about Riversimple's approach is the total coherence of its vision: to provide sustainable personal transport as a service rather than a product. This switches the incentive from 'sell a short-lived car for maximum money' to 'design and build a long-lived car that has low running costs'. Using fuel cells, Riversimple's vehicle achieves the equivalent of 300mpg and well-to-wheel emissions of 31g CO_2/km. Design is open-sourced, production is small scale and local and the entire co-owned business model rewards the minimisation of resource consumption and environmental impact. We need more thinking like this." — MA

riversimple.com

IMAGE © RIVERSIMPLE LLP

Riversimple provides access to highly efficient hydrogen vehicles for personal transport. The world's first commercially viable hydrogen car, Riversimple could reduce the environmental impact of personal cars. The vehicle itself is just one of seven mutually reinforcing strategies, which come together to form the business model and company bedrock. One of the key tenets is that Riversimple vehicles cannot be bought or owned, but are always leased from the company for a specific duration. Riversimple has been developed using a whole system design approach, optimising the entire product and service offer rather than individual elements. This has enabled a five-fold increase in efficiency over typical vehicles, while the business model is expected to ensure a commercially viable introduction to market. The business model and 60 production prototypes will both be piloted in 2012.

VANMOOF No 5

Designed by VANMOOF

☆ Nominated by ANTOINETTE KLAWER: "You would think that improving the design of the urban Dutch bicycle after 130 years of evolution was not possible, but each year numerous inventions and modernisations still broaden our horizons. One outstanding design of 2010 is the VANMOOF No 5. The bike incorporates equipment which makes it almost impossible to steal or damage it. The LED lights and gear cables are hidden within the frame, preventing the cables from breaking or getting stuck in a neighbour's bike and the brakes and lock are incorporated for the same reason. Giving the bike a tough and sophisticated look did not make it unaffordably expensive. Half the price of some competitors, the VANMOOF No 5 brings stylish city transport within everybody's reach." — AK

vanmoof.com

IMAGE © VANMOOF

VANMOOF No 5 is a no-nonsense bicycle where simplicity is key. Designed with the modern city and commuter in mind, its wireless frame is stripped of all non-essential items and made from lightweight, rust-free aluminium. The slightly oversized frame tubes give the bike its distinctive look, provide the rigidity needed for practical use and also create a space to secrete the clever ideas hidden within. A high quality ABUS lock is embedded within the bicycle, accessed by turning a key in the frame and pulling the chain out from inside. Strong LED lamps are also built-in and are rechargeable through solar power or a USB port.

YIKEBIKE

Designed by GRANT RYAN

☆ Nominated by DALE HARROW // ANDREW NAHUM:
"Electric bikes are generally heavy, more ungainly and inelegant versions of conventional bikes, and they are equally vulnerable to theft and difficult to store. YikeBike is a total reinvention of the electric two-wheeler, creating a portable personal solution that can accompany the owner anywhere. It is, in effect, the 'iPod of personal mobility' and has the potential to revolutionise urban travel. The carbon fibre folding bike is light and small enough to be taken into home or work and stowed easily. Many regard it as the most interesting development in two-wheeled transport in decades, certainly since the Honda 50 or perhaps the Brompton folding bike." — AN

yikebike.com

IMAGE © YIKEBIKE LTD

YikeBike was created by a team of engineers and entrepreneurs who wanted to dramatically change urban transport. Providing city dwellers with a fast, safe and easy way to navigate their environment, YikeBike is the smallest and lightest electric folding bike in the world. The carbon fibre construction means it can be carried on buses and trains, lifted up stairs or easily stored under a desk or in a cupboard. The battery can be charged in just 30 minutes, powering a range of 10km. YikeBike's mini-farthing design provides a radically different, upright, riding position, with the handlebars situated behind the rider. This steering and wheel configuration delivers a safe and smooth ride, with greater visibility than a traditional bike.

NOMINATORS

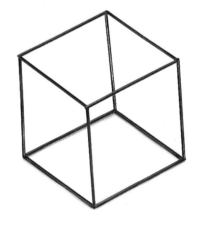

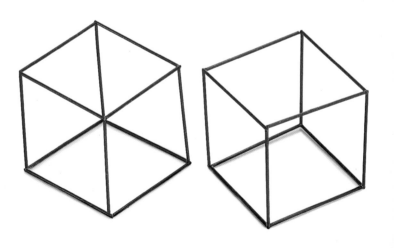

☆ MARK ADAMS is managing director of Vitsœ, the company that has made Dieter Rams' furniture for 50 years. After succeeding Niels Vitsœ, Adams relocated the company to Britain and expanded it worldwide. A zoologist, he is a passionate advocate for the world to live better, with less that lasts longer, and speaks widely on this and related topics.

☆ ED ANNINK is a Netherlands-based designer, curator and the co-founder and owner of Ontwerpwerk multidisciplinary design in Den Haag. He has recently published Gerd Arntz: Graphic Designer, Norm=Form, about standardisation and design, and The Style of the State, about the visual identity of the Dutch Government.

☆ PAOLA ANTONELLI is senior curator at the Department of Architecture & Design at The Museum of Modern Art. Through her exhibitions, teachings and writing, Paola strives to promote a deeper understanding of design's transformative and constructive influence on the world. She is working on several exhibition ideas and on the book Design Bites, about basic foods taken as examples of outstanding design.

☆ ALEX BEC is director of It's Nice That, a London-based studio focused on championing creativity. Through It's Nice That Alex has been responsible for co-editing printed publications and online content, organising events and art directing commercial work for some of the world's biggest brands.

☆ ADELIA BORGES is a design curator and writer based in Brazil. Formerly director of the Brazilian House Museum, she has written six books on design and frequently contributes to the international press. Adélia is interested in design and crafts as a tool for social change, especially in the southern hemisphere.

☆ LUCY BULLIVANT is an architectural curator, critic and author whose books include Masterplanning Futures, Anglo Files, Responsive Environments, 4dspace and 4dsocial. She is a correspondent for Domus, The Plan, Volume and Indesign and curated Give Me More Green In-Between for the 2010 London Festival of Architecture. In 2010 she was elected an Honorary Fellow of RIBA.

☆ PATRICK BURGOYNE has been the editor of Creative Review magazine since 1999. He is the author of several books on design and visual culture and has written for publications including the Independent, Graphis and La Repubblica.

☆ IAN CARTLIDGE is co-founder of design consultancy Cartlidge Levene. Ian has been responsible for award-winning wayfinding and environmental graphics projects including the Barbican Arts Centre, Selfridges, the V&A and the Guardian, News and Media. Cartlidge Levene's long association with the Design Museum continued with the 2010 Brit Insurance Designs of the Year exhibition. Ian is currently working on major wayfinding projects for Tate Modern and Musée d'Art de Nantes.

☆ DANIEL CHARNY is a curator, designer and tutor with an industrial design background. Co-founder of creative projects consultancy From Now On, he is a strategic consultant and guest curator for the Design Museum, London and senior tutor at the Royal College of Art. In 2002 he started The Aram Gallery for experimental and new work.

☆ ARIC CHEN is a Beijing and New York-based writer, critic and curator specialising in design, architecture and art. A frequent contributor to The New York Times, Wallpaper* and others, he was recently appointed creative director of a new Beijing Design Week that will launch in 2011.

☆ SEBASTIAN CONRAN is director of Sebastian Conran Associates, focusing on product, branding and user experience design, and visiting professor of design against crime at Central Saint Martins. He has written numerous books and papers on design, taught at the Royal College of Art, where he is an Honorary Fellow, and judges many international awards such as D&AD, Red Dot, and Design Week. He is also a founding trustee of the Design Museum.

☆ BRONWYN COSGRAVE is a London-based writer, curator and creative consultant to luxury brands. She is founding chairperson of the Dorchester Collection Fashion Prize and author of Made For Each Other, Fashion and the Academy Awards, the first fashion history of the Oscars. She contributes to the Daily Telegraph and the international editions of Vanity Fair and Vogue.

☆ JAMES DYSON discovered industrial design at the Royal College of Art. He invented dual cyclone™ technology in 1979, after growing frustrated by the loss of suction in vacuum cleaner bags. James continues to work alongside his team of engineers and scientists developing new technologies to overcome everyday frustrations – including the Dyson Air Multiplier fan and the Dyson Airblade hand dryer.

☆ SIMON ESTERSON is a London-based editorial designer. He is art director of Eye, the international review of graphic design.

☆ THOMAS GEISLER is design curator at the Museum of Applied Arts/Contemporary Arts (MAK) in Vienna and co-founder of Neigungsgruppe Design and Vienna Design Week. As a senior scientist at the Department of Design History and Theory he was instrumental in establishing the Victor J. Papanek Foundation at the University of Applied Arts Vienna.

☆ DEE HALLIGAN is a commissioning producer and project manager whose past projects include exhibitions for the Science Museum, the redesign of Marks & Spencer stores and Tate Galleries' digital strategy. She is co-founder of the creative projects consultancy From Now On.

☆ ANNA THORUD HAMMER is managing director of DogA, The Norwegian Centre for Design and Architecture.

☆ DALE HARROW is professor of vehicle design at the Royal College of Art and director of the college's global centre of excellence in automotive design education. He has collaborated with many automotive and design companies including Seymour Powell, Pentagram, Yamaha, Honda, Sony and Tefal.

☆ SAM HECHT is co-founder of the London-based design office, Industrial Facility. He was appointed Royal Designer for Industry in 2008 and is visiting professor at HfG Karlsruhe, Germany.

☆ WAYNE HEMINGWAY MBE co-founded the successful fashion brand Red or Dead and is now a partner in HemingwayDesign specialising in affordable housing and social design. His new project, the Vintage Festival, an annual celebration of British creativity, is currently attracting international attention.

☆ WILL HUDSON is founder and director of It's Nice That, a London-based studio focused on championing creativity. Through It's Nice That Will has been responsible for curating online content, co-editing printed publications and organising events, as well as art directing commercial work for brands of all sizes.

☆ CATHERINE INCE is a curator at the Barbican Art Gallery in London specialising in design and architecture. Previously, she worked for the British Council where she organised the British Pavilion at the 2006 and 2008 Venice Architecture Biennales as well as an international exhibitions and events programme.

☆ MATT JONES is a director at BERG Ltd, a London-based design and invention company. He has been design director for Nokia, Sapient and BBC News and co-founded Dopplr.com, which was recently acquired by Nokia. He is a visiting tutor on the design interactions course at the Royal College of Art, and writes on design and other things at magicalnihilism.com.

☆ DAVID KESTER is chief executive of the Design Council, which promotes and demonstrates the value of design. He is a council member of the Royal College of Art and the RSA and a board member of the Design Business Association. He is a regular commentator and advisor to government on the creative economy, enterprise and innovation.

☆ ANTOINETTE KLAWER is a Netherlands-based independent project manager specialising in international travelling design exhibitions. She is currently project manager of the Dutch Design Awards travelling exhibition and Design Academy Eindhoven exhibitions.

☆ JEREMY LESLIE is creative director of magCulture. As well as hands-on design, magCulture provides consultancy and advice to publishers and, increasingly, other clients working with content for print and digital media. He is a passionate advocate for editorial design, regularly contributing to the creative press and international design conferences, and blogging at magCulture.com/blog.

☆ ALISON MOLONEY is a curator and project manager for the British Council's Design and Architecture department and is the organisation's leading fashion expert. She is currently London-based but has also worked on the Arabian Peninsula as head of arts for the British Council's Middle East region.

☆ ANDREW NAHUM is principal curator of technology and engineering at the Science Museum, London and author of the Design Museum's recent title, Fifty cars that changed the world. He has written extensively on the history of technology, aviation and transport and he is currently completing a technological and economic study of the British aircraft industry in the years following the Second World War.

☆ GUY NORDENSON is a practising structural engineer in New York and professor of structural engineering and architecture at Princeton University. He co-curated MoMa's 2004 Tall Buildings exhibition and his research and book On the Water | Palisade Bay inspired the MoMA Rising Currents workshop and exhibition in 2010. His book Patterns and Structure: Selected Writings 1973-2008 was recently published by Lars Muller.

☆ MICHELLE OGUNDEHIN is editor in chief of ELLE Decoration, a trustee of the V&A Museum and director of the MO:Studio design consultancy. She has written for a wide range of newspapers and magazines and worked with major brands including Benetton, Harvey Nichols, Selfridges and Habitat.

☆ BRIAN PARKES has been director at JamFactory Contemporary Craft and Design in Adelaide since April 2010. Previously he spent ten years as associate director at Object Gallery in Sydney where he curated several important exhibitions, including the landmark survey of Australian design, Freestyle: new Australian design for living.

☆ ROSS PHILLIPS is an award-winning interaction designer. Recent projects include site-specific installations for Nokia and Jimmy Choo, Mirror Mirror for Topshop (with SHOWstudio.com) and Videogrid for Decode at the V&A Museum. He currently works as a consultant for English luxury company Mulberry and produces interactive commissions for public spaces and brands.

☆ FRANCESCA PICCHI is an architect and a journalist for Domus magazine, Italy.

☆ PAULA REED is style director of Grazia and has previously worked on the Sunday Times, Harpers & Queen and Condé Nast Traveller. She is a regular on TV's Project Catwalk and 10 Years Younger and is the author of Style Clinic.

☆ LYNDA RELPH-KNIGHT has been editor of Design Week, the world's only weekly design magazine, for over two decades. She is a fellow of the RSA and an honorary fellow of the Royal College of Art.

☆ CAROLINE ROUX is a London-based design writer and consultant. She contributes to a range of titles including the Independent, the Financial Times, Harper's Bazaar, Fantastic Man and Pin Up.

☆ DAVID ROWAN is the editor of Wired UK. He writes the Digital Life column in GQ magazine and the Tech Traveller column in Condé Nast Traveller. He has edited the Guardian's websites, been a columnist for The Times, and made TV films for Channel 4 News.

☆ RAYMUND RYAN is curator of the Heinz Architectural Center at Pittsburgh's Carnegie Museum of Art. Recent exhibitions include Laboratory of Architecture/ Fernando Romero, Gritty Brits: New London Architecture, and Frank Lloyd Wright: Renewing the Legacy. He has served as Ireland's commissioner for the Venice Architecture Biennale and contributed to journals worldwide.

☆ ZOE RYAN is a British curator and writer. She is currently acting chair of the Department of Architecture and Design and Neville Bryan curator of design at the Art Institute of Chicago as well as adjunct assistant professor at the School of Art and Design, University of Illinois at Chicago. She is regularly called upon as a lecturer, critic and juror and her writing on architecture and design has been published internationally.

☆ DALJIT SINGH is founder of the Digit digital agency and executive creative director of Conran Singh, a new interactive design agency within the Conran Group. He recently joined the International Academy of Digital Arts and has been featured in the Financial Times' Top 50 Creative Minds.

☆ CYNTHIA E SMITH is curator of socially responsible design at Cooper-Hewitt, National Design Museum, Smithsonian Institution. She curated Design for the Other 90% (2007), co-curated the National Design Triennial: Why Design Now? (2010) and is currently working on Design with the Other 90%: Cities, scheduled to open in New York in October 2011.

☆ SONNET STANFILL is an author, lecturer and curator of twentieth-century and contemporary fashion at the V&A. She curated New York Fashion Now (2007), Ossie Clark (2003) and is currently researching a display devoted to London fashion in the 1980s.

☆ HENRIETTA THOMPSON
is a journalist, author and
curator, and editor-at-large
for Wallpaper*. Specialising in
design, architecture, culture and
innovation, she is based in London.

☆ HUIB HAYE VAN DER WERF
is a Netherlands-based writer
and curator with a background
in contemporary visual arts
and art in public spaces. He is
a curator for the Netherlands
Architecture Institute (NAi) in
Rotterdam and participates in art
and design advisory committees
for The Hague and Utrecht.
He is also a member of the
National Foundation for Visual
Arts, Design and Architecture.

☆ SHANE WALTER is a creative
director, curator, writer and
producer. He co-founded
onedotzero, the global digital
art and design organisation, and
onedotzero industries, where he
produces and consults for the
world's best-known brands and
bands. He has authored three
books and co-curated Decode:
Digital Design Sensations at the
V&A Museum and CAFA Beijing.

☆ SARAH WEIR is head of arts
and cultural strategy for the
London 2012 Olympic Delivery
Authority. After a 15 year career
in business, Sarah moved into the
arts, with roles at Purdy Hicks
Gallery, Arts and Business and the
Royal Academy of Arts. She has
also held executive director roles
with the Arts Council England
and the Almeida Theatre.

☆ GARETH WILLIAMS is senior
tutor of design products at the
Royal College of Art, London.

☆ JANE WITHERS is a design
consultant, curator and writer
based in London. She curated
In Praise of Shadows, on new
lighting design, at the V&A (2009)
and 1% Water at Z33 (2008).
She has written several books
on design and architecture, and
regularly teaches and speaks
on design internationally.

PAST
WINNERS

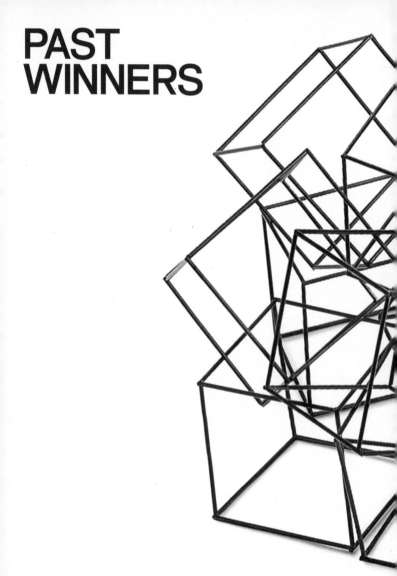

BRIT INSURANCE
AWARD WINNERS 2010

OVERALL WINNER of BRIT INSURANCE DESIGN AWARD 2010
Category winner PRODUCT
FOLDING PLUG [UK] by **MIN-KYU CHOI**

Category winner ARCHITECTURE
MONTERREY HOUSING [MEXICO] by **ELEMENTAL S.A., CHILE**

Category winner FASHION
**ALEXANDER MCQUEEN SPRING/SUMMER '10 // SPRING/SUMMER '10
CATWALK PRESENTATION, PLATO'S ATLANTIS** [UK]
by **ALEXANDER MCQUEEN**

Category winner FURNITURE
GRASSWORKS [NETHERLANDS] by **JAIR STRASCHNOW**

Category winner GRAPHICS
THE NEWSPAPER CLUB [UK] by **BEN TERRETT // RUSSELL DAVIES //
TOM TAYLOR**

Category winner INTERACTIVE
THE EYEWRITER [USA] developed by members of **FREE ART AND
TECHNOLOGY // OPEN FRAMEWORKS // GRAFFITI RESEARCH LAB //
THE EBELING GROUP // TONY QUAN**

Category winner TRANSPORT
E430 ELECTRIC AIRCRAFT [CHINA] by **YUNEEC INTERNATIONAL**

IMAGE © MIN-KYU CHOI

BRIT INSURANCE
AWARD WINNERS 2009

OVERALL WINNER of BRIT INSURANCE DESIGN AWARD 2009
Category winner GRAPHICS
BARACK OBAMA POSTER [USA] by **SHEPARD FAIREY**

Category winner ARCHITECTURE
NEW OSLO OPERA HOUSE [NORWAY] by **SNØHETTA**

Category winner FASHION
A BLACK ISSUE JULY 2008 [ITALY] by **VOGUE ITALIA**

Category winner FURNITURE
MYTO CHAIR [ITALY] by **KONSTANTIN GRCIC**

Category winner INTERACTIVE
MAKE MAGAZINE [USA] published by **O'REILLY**

Category winner PRODUCT
MAGNO WOODEN RADIO [INDONESIA] by **SINGGIH S KARTONO**

Category winner TRANSPORT
LINE-J MEDELLIN METRO CABLE [COLOMBIA] by **POMA FRANCE**

IMAGE © SHEPARD FAIREY

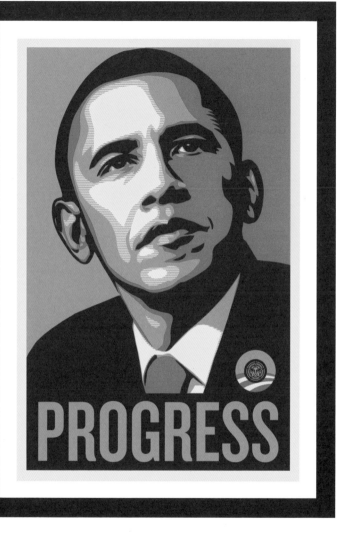

BRIT INSURANCE
AWARD WINNERS 2008

OVERALL WINNER of BRIT INSURANCE DESIGN AWARD 2008
Category winner PRODUCT
ONE LAPTOP PER CHILD [USA] by **YVES BEHAR** of **FUSEPROJECT**

Category winner ARCHITECTURE
THE MAIN STADIUM FOR THE 2008 OLYMPIC GAMES, BEIJING [CHINA]
by **HERZOG & DE MEURON ARCHITECTS**

Category winner FASHION
AIRBORNE, AUTUMN/WINTER '07 [UK] by **HUSSEIN CHALAYAN**

Category winner FURNITURE
100 CHAIRS IN 100 DAYS [UK] by **MARTINO GAMPER**

Category winner GRAPHICS
PENGUIN CLASSICS DELUXE EDITION [USA] by various artists
for the **PENGUIN GROUP**

Category winner INTERACTIVE
BURBLE LONDON [UK] by **HAQUE DESIGN+RESEARCH LIMITED**
with **SETH GARLOCK // ROLF PIXEY**

Category winner TRANSPORT
MEX-X WHEELCHAIR FOR CHILDREN [GERMANY] by **MEYRA-ORTOPEDIA**

IMAGE © FUSEPROJECT

Text set in DM NEWS GOTHIC CONDENSED Regular // Bold © ROBERT GREEN
Titles set in DM SCHULBUCH Demi // Bold © GRAPHIC THOUGHT FACILITY
Cover stock COLORPLAN PRISTINE WHITE BUCKRAM 270 g/m²
Text stock MOHAWK OPTIONS PC100 118 g/m²
Stock supplied by GF SMITH, LONDON
Printing, reprographics, binding and finishing by THE COLOURHOUSE, LONDON